Richard Wilton

Lyrics: Sylvan and Sacred

Richard Wilton

Lyrics: Sylvan and Sacred

ISBN/EAN: 9783744792677

Printed in Europe, USA, Canada, Australia, Japan

Cover: Foto ©Thomas Meinert / pixelio.de

More available books at **www.hansebooks.com**

LYRICS:

SYLVAN AND SACRED.

BY

THE REV. RICHARD WILTON, M.A.,
ST. CATHARINE'S COLLEGE, CAMBRIDGE.
Author of "Wood-Notes and Church-Bells."

Here sylvan touches brighten sacred lays:
Nature lends colour, Grace melodious praise.

LONDON:
GEORGE BELL & SONS, YORK STREET, COVENT GARDEN.
1878.

To

The Right Honourable and Most Reverend

William Thomson, D.D.,

Lord Archbishop of York,

This Volume is, by His Grace's kind permission,

Respectfully dedicated.

If in the multitude of public cares
  And lofty duties which attend thy way,
    Thine hand perchance should hold a blooming spray,
Which lately fluttered in sweet morning airs;
Touched by the fragrant message that it bears
  From peaceful solitudes, thou mightest say,
    'A simple flower can cheer the burdened day,
And rest the wearied spirit unawares:'
Then for a poet's privilege I pray,
  To place this garland underneath thine eye,
Fresh from the fields and woods in which I stray;
  Ambitious that amid thy labours high
Haply the blossom of some rural lay
  Might waken soothing thoughts of earth or sky.

CONTENTS.

	PAGE
Dedicatory Sonnet to the Archbishop of York	v
Introductory Rondeau	xv
The Hawthorn and the Wild Rose	1
The Swallow	2
Grace	3
Evening Rest	6
The Wind at Midnight	7
Starlight	8
Signs of Summer	9
The Voice of Our Churches	13
The Plain of York from the Yorkshire Wolds	14
Now or When	15
Patrington Church	16
The Shepherd's Reed	17
On a Copy of Leonardo da Vinci's "Last Supper"	19
'The Shadow of Death'	20
Milton's Portrait	21
Beech-Leaves, Snow, and Violets	22
Flamborough Lighthouse	25
An Autumn Day at Fountains' Abbey	26
On the View of Faringford, the Poet Laureate's Home	27
On the New Church Spire at Grasby, in connection with the Poetry of Charles Tennyson Turner	28
To Mrs. Charles Tennyson Turner	29
To Some Friends About to Winter at Canea, in Crete	30

CONTENTS.

	PAGE
To a Friend Starting for Palestine	31
A Sylvan Nook, Londesborough Park	32
Winter-Berries	36
The Arrow-Seed; or, Sowing Unawares	37
The Victim and the Priest	38
The Kingfisher; or, A Happy Wedding Omen	41
The Birds' First Halting-Place	42
Butterflies	43
A Time of Refreshing	44
Glen Cripesdale, Loch Sunart	46
On a Highland Burying-Place	47
Kinloch Waterfall	48
Loch Teachus	49
The Highland Shepherd	50
The Cross and the Aspen Tree	51
The Lifting of the Mist	52
Mount Glamaig, Isle of Skye	53
The Garden of the Soul	54

SONNETS ON THE FATHERS.

Ignatius	57
Polycarp	58
Justin Martyr	59
Tertullian	60
Irenæus	61
Origen	62
Eusebius	63
Athanasius	64

Snowdrops	65
The Cross and the Moss	67
My Painted Window	68
Christmas Fare for the Birds	69
A Prayer for the New Year	70

CONTENTS.

	PAGE
Thoughts for New Year's Day.—The Circumcision of Christ	71
Palm Sunday	74
Lent; or, The Shadow of the Cross	78
Good Friday. A Coincidence	79
Easter Day	80
A Prayer for Whitsuntide	84
Christmas Day	87
Machœrus	90
Livingstone's Last Prayer	91
On the Death upon Snowdon of Frederick R. Wilton, B.A., in the year 1874	92
At His Feet	93
The Christian Life	96
Revolving Years	97
Searching the Scriptures	98

SONNETS ON THE TYPES.

The Brazen Altar	99
The Laver or Molten Sea	100
The Golden Candlestick	101
The Table of Shewbread	102
The Veil of the Temple	103
Manna	104
The Brazen Serpent	105
The Hyssop	106
The Red Heifer	107
The Scapegoat	108
The Paschal Lamb	109

"Let Us Pass Over to the Other Side"	110
Mansions of Heaven and Earth	112
On the Morning Star	113
Heavenly Silence	114

CONTENTS.

	PAGE
The First Violet	115
On the Baptism of Our Infant	117
Mabel's Hat	118
Crab-apple Gatherers	119
Harvest Praise	120
Church Sculpture	123
A Cruciform Church	124
Water Turned to Wine	125
Solace in Sickness	128
A Suffering Christian's Prayer	129
The Rainbow at Sunset	130
Home and Heaven	131
Winter Lessons	132
A Gethsemane Marigold	134
On a Cypress from Mount Sinai	135
On a Denarius of Tiberius Cæsar	136
The Temple Windows	137
"Meet for the Master's Use"	138
The Curfew	140
Hilda's Wood, Hackness, near Scarborough	141
On an Old Ash Tree in Londesborough Park	142
Autumn Leaves	143
The Bird-Comforter	146
Hope for Old Age	147
Auburn, a Seaside Elegy	148
Paradise	151
Samson's Riddle	152
On Hearing the Chiff-Chaff	153
On a Thrush Singing at a Funeral in November	156
A Thought in a March Rookery	157
Passing Away	158
Undersongs	159

CONTENTS.   xi

	PAGE
The Pillar	160
The Roman Camp, Cawthorne, near Pickering	163
On the Sight of a Sea-bird in April	164
A White Christmas	165
A Little Girl at the Seaside	166
The Rainbow, a Symbol	169
Take up and Read	170
Winter Wheat	171
Winter Blossoms	172
From My Study Window	173
Iona	179
Olive Trees in Gethsemane	180
The Last Communion, a Parish Incident	181
Warp and Woof	182
On a Photograph	183

RONDEAUX.

Sweet Eglantine	184
In Twilight Dim	185
In Sunshine Sweet	186
Dorothea	187
The East Window in York Minster	188
The Sanctuary	189
My Father worketh hitherto	190
Blue Hyacinths	191
Sweet, soft, and low	192
"Till my Change come"	193

TRANSLATIONS FROM GEORGE HERBERT.

George Herbert's Description of his Mother	197
On the Reed, Crown of Thorns, etc.	201
On the Scourge	202
On the Parted Garments	202
On the Penitent Thief	203

CONTENTS.

	PAGE
TRANSLATIONS FROM GEORGE HERBERT, (*continued.*)	
On Christ about to ascend the Cross	203
Christ on the Cross	204
On the Nails	204
On the bowed Head	205
The Open Graves	205
The Rent Rocks	206
Man an Image	207
The Fatherland	207
On Stephen Stoned	208
On Simon Magus	208
Affliction	209
On the Angels	209
On a Sundial	210
To John on the Breast of Christ	211
To the Lord	211
TRANSLATIONS FROM RICHARD CRASHAW.	
The Infant Christ presented in the Temple	215
On the Day of the Lord's Ascension	216
On the Cloud which received the Lord	216
On the Descent of the Holy Spirit	217
From Description of Human Life	218
Jesus Christ's Expostulation with an Ungrateful World	219
Christ All, Alone, in all things	220
Concluding Rondeau	221

LYRICS:

SYLVAN AND SACRED.

To the Reader.

In wood and lane I wander free
And gather flowers from bank or tree;
And with a loving hand entwine
The hawthorn, rose, and eglantine;
And here I bring the wreath to thee.

Thy happy lot it may not be
To see the lark spring from the lea;
Or breathe the dewy odours fine
In wood and lane.

But there are other fields Divine,
Which in dim city may be thine;
Where thou the Flower of flowers mayst see,
And catch the Spirit's melody;
Nor thine alone, but also mine
In wood and lane.

Londesborough Rectory,
   East Yorkshire, 1878.

THE HAWTHORN AND THE WILD ROSE.

I learnt a lesson from the flowers to-day:—
   As o'er the fading hawthorn-blooms I sighed,
   Whose petals fair lay scattered far and wide;
Lo, suddenly upon a dancing spray
I saw the first wild-roses clustered gay.
   What though the smile I loved, so soon had died
   From one sweet flower—there, shining at its side,
The blushing Rose surpassed the snowy May.
So, if as life glides on, we miss some flowers
   Which once shed light and fragrance on our way,
Yet still the kindly-compensating hours
   Weave us fresh wreaths in beautiful array;
   And long as in the paths of peace we stay,
Successive benedictions shall be ours!

THE SWALLOW.

O Swallow, Summer reigns within thy heart,
    As sunshine sleeps upon thy purple wing;
    For lo! thou comest with the brightening Spring,
And yellowing Autumn warns thee to depart.
To wait on thy king's march is all thine art,
    And to his flowery train, rejoicing, cling;
    While tidings of his glory thou dost bring
Where'er thine arrowy form is seen to dart.
Oh, that Heaven's Summer in my heart might rest,
    And cheering rays about me I might fling,
Blessing all others while myself am blest;
    Then I must follow too my viewless King,
And catch from Him the sunshine of the breast,
    And round me flowers will smile and birds will sing.

GRACE.

The snowdrop round it throws
  A bright and cheery smile,
But lingers like the snows
  A very little while.

The violet lifts its head
  And sweetly looks around,
But soon its bloom is shed,
  Its fragrance is not found.

The yellow primrose peeps
  In many a sheltered lane,
But soon to darkness creeps:
  We seek its light in vain.

LYRICS:

Not so with Heavenly Grace:
    Wherever it takes root,
It holds its steadfast place
    And blossoms into fruit.

Its vesture is Divine;
    A snowdrop white and fair,
Grace comes from Heaven to shine
    In this terrestrial air.

But still it keeps its eye
    Fixed on yon arch of blue,
And catches from the sky
    A soft celestial hue.

And soon it will behold
    Awaiting it above
A crown of lustrous gold
    Wreathed with immortal love.

Lord, plant Thy grace in me;
  So all the world will own,
When once the flower they see
  That Thou the seed hast sown.

EVENING REST.

The sun sinks slowly in the crimson West,
   And waves the welcome signal of repose;
   His ploughshare left i' the furrow, the hind goes
With his tired horses to accustomed rest.
To yon tall trees, tufted with many a nest,
   The rooks sail o'er the sky: the ringdove knows
   His firry roosting-place at daylight's close:
Each creature with some sheltered nook is blest.
And as I too turn to my peaceful home,
   Where gentle greetings solace toil and care,
I think of One content awhile to roam
   An Exile from high Heav'n; who "had not where
To lay His head"—He, and He only, found
Whose busy days no restful evening crowned.

THE WIND AT MIDNIGHT.

O wind, that moanest at the midnight hour
  Around my chamber, what is thy desire?
  Now whispering low and ready to expire,
Now waxing louder with a fitful power.
What wouldest thou? Whence thy mysterious dower
  To thrill the darkness like a trembling lyre;
  Or wake sweet music, now far off, now nigher,
As of some heavenly bird in secret bower?
O Wind, O Bird, I know Thee whence Thou camest,
  And what soft message lurks beneath Thy wing:
When earth is hushed in silence, then Thou claimest
  With plaintive tones an audience for the King:
Speak, Lord, I hear—Oh, let Thy Holy Dove
Soothe my lone heart with whispers of Thy love.

LYRICS:

STARLIGHT.

At midnight, when yon azure fields on high
  Sparkle and glow without one cloudy bar,
  The radiance of some "bright particular star"
Attracts, perchance, and holds my watching eye.
That star may long have vanished from the sky;
  Yet still its unspent rays, borne from afar,
  Come darting downwards in their golden car—
Proof it once glittered in the galaxy.
So in my heart I feel a healing ray
  Sweetly transmitted from a Star divine,
  Which once illumed the coasts of Palestine:
And though its beauty beams not there to-day,
  I know that Star of old did truly shine,
  Because its cheering radiance now is mine.

SIGNS OF SUMMER.

'And He spake to them a parable; Behold the fig-tree, and all the trees; when they now shoot forth' ('when his branch is yet tender, and putteth forth leaves'—S. Matt. xxiv. 32), 'ye see and know of your own selves that summer is now nigh at hand. So likewise ye, when ye see these things come to pass, know ye that the kingdom of God is nigh at hand' ('even at the doors'—S. Matt.).—S. LUKE xxi. 29-31.

On the fig-tree vernal
    And on 'all the trees,'
Precious fruit eternal
    Faith's keen vision sees.

When the branch is tender,
    And the budding stem;
And each shootlet slender
    Shows its emerald gem;

Then ye know that Summer
    Must be very near,
With each bright new-comer
    Of the full-blown year.

Soon the punctual swallow,
    And the turtle's voice,
On soft wings will follow,
    Bidding earth rejoice;

Morns of dewy pleasure
    Scatter blooms around,
Beauty without measure,
    Gladness without bound.

So when every token
    In the earth and sky,
Which the Lord hath spoken
    Meets your watching eye;

Then, ye may be certain,
   Dawns the day of doom;
He will rend the curtain,
   And His Kingdom come.

Yet to saints, remember,
   That decisive day
Comes, not like December,
   Clad in stern array,

But in all the glory
   Of a Summer-noon—
Songs and painted story
   Of the flowery June.

Oh, the joy, the singing!
   Oh, the fadeless blooms!
Summer-gladness bringing—
   When His Kingdom comes.

Now, Lord, send Thy Spirit
To my wintry breast—
Pledge I shall inherit
That celestial rest,

Those sweet songs and roses
In Thy Kingdom fair,
Where Thy Church reposes
Fanned with Summer air!

THE VOICE OF OUR CHURCHES.

SUGGESTED BY THE ARCHBISHOP OF YORK'S SERMON AT THE RE-OPENING OF THE SOUTH TRANSEPT OF YORK MINSTER.

"Abide with us, O Lord, our heart's desire,
  For shadows gather round earth's evening hour."
  Such voice, methinks, goes up from Minster tower,
From village steeple and from city spire,
Loud-clashing belfry and harmonious choir.
  To Heaven they speak with an appealing power,
  Our myriad churches, shining with the dower
Of Art's adornments, and Devotion's fire.
"Abide with us!" unceasingly they cry,
  "As through the ages past. The world grows old:
  The love of many waxes faint and cold:
But still we lift our faithful hands on high,
And feeling after Thee up the dim sky,
  Upon Thy cloudy skirts would fain lay hold!"

THE PLAIN OF YORK
FROM THE YORKSHIRE WOLDS.

We gazed upon a mighty sunlit plain
   Which swept, to right and left, the horizon's bound:
   In its wide arms was many a battle-ground,
But at its heart a glorious Minster-fane.
The sky was bright, and a melodious rain
   Fell from the soaring larks, with silvery sound:
   No note of discord in the air was found,
Nor on the landscape's face one marring stain.
Thus, while we sojourn in this world of strife
   May love to God be still the central thought
Which sweetly rules and permeates our life:
   Thus, may our soul with light and peace be fraught,
And all our days with grateful music rife—
   An echo from angelic voices caught!

NOW OR WHEN,

BEING THE LEGEND OF A SUNDIAL ON BEVERLEY MINSTER.

On the tall buttress of a Minster grey,
   The glorious work of long-forgotten men,
   I read this Dial-legend,—"Now or When."
Well had these builders used their little day
Of service—witness this sublime display
   Of blossomed stone, dazzling the gazer's ken.
   These towers attest they knew 'twas there and then,
Not some vague morrow they must work and pray.
Oh, let us seize this transitory NOW
   From which to build a life-work that will last:
In humble prayer and worship let us bow
   Ere fleeting opportunity is past.
When once Life's sun forsakes the Dial-plate,
For work and for repentance 'tis too late!

PATRINGTON CHURCH.

"THE QUEEN OF HOLDERNESS."

They toiled the God of Heaven to glorify
  With lavish ornament of nave and choir,
  And lofty tower that shoots into a spire
Of queenly grace, conspicuous far and nigh.
But lo! that slender shaft against the sky,
  Rosed by the dawn or tipped with sunset fire—
  Of home-bound sailors is the dear desire
And through the shoals of Humber guides their eye.
Those patient builders reared a stately shrine
  For the sweet sacrifice of praise and prayer,
And earthly use grew from a work divine;
  So the pure life that breathes celestial air
And points to Heaven, for man will also shine,
  A star of comfort 'mid the waves of care!

THE SHEPHERD'S REED.

"And the Lord said, Whereunto then shall I liken the men of this generation? And to what are they like? They are like unto children sitting in the market place, and calling one to another; and saying, We have piped unto you, and ye have not danced; we have mourned unto you, and ye have not wept. For John the Baptist came neither eating bread nor drinking wine; and ye say, He hath a devil. The Son of Man is come eating and drinking; and ye say, Behold a gluttonous man and a winebibber, a friend of publicans and sinners."—S. LUKE vii. 31-34.

O Son of Man, great Shepherd of the sheep,
Thou pipest to us, shall Thy children weep?
Sheep of Thy pasture, shall we not rejoice,
And dance to Thy soft notes and gentle voice?

No strain so sweet e'er flowed from Grecian lute,
Or pipe of Arcady, or Dorian flute;
Of Roman lyre no mention shall be made,
And David's harp before this reed must fade.

A simple reed by Syrian waters found
From human lips took a celestial sound;
Through it strange melodies our Shepherd blew,
And wondering, wistful ones around Him drew.

Of heavenly love with cadence deep it told,
Of labours long to win them to the fold,
Of bleeding feet upon the mountains steep,
And life laid down to save His erring sheep.

O loving Shepherd, to that gracious strain
We listen and we listen once again,
And while its music sinks into our heart,
Our fears grow fainter and our doubts depart.

Lord, pipe to me, and I will weep no more,
But joyful follow to yon happy shore,
Where my glad soul shall sing and dance to Thee
In the "green pastures" of Eternity!

ON THE LARGE COPY PAINTED BY SELOUS OF LEONARDO DA VINCI'S "LAST SUPPER,"

IN THE DINING-ROOM OF MY FRIEND, THE REV. C. F. NORMAN, MISTLEY PLACE, MANNINGTREE.

No shadow falls upon the festive room
   From that pathetic scene—that clouded Face
   Bent on the board with melancholy grace.
That glorious picture sheds no touch of gloom,
But rather a soft radiance to illume
   The banquet, as upon the wall we trace
   The symbol of a happier time and place,
When at Heaven's feast immortal flowers shall bloom.
"Jesus and His disciples" let us "call"
   To bless and beautify our brightest hours,
And breathe a chastened gladness over all:
   Thus will He call us to those festal bowers,
Where no fair pictured form shall meet the view,
But His own Self—the Living, Loving, True.

'THE SHADOW OF DEATH.'

SUGGESTED BY MR. HOLMAN HUNT'S FAMOUS PICTURE.

The 'twelve hours' of Thy 'day' of toil are fled,
  O glorious Workman; and the gorgeous West
  And level shadows bid to evening rest:
Thy weary arms to right and left are spread,
As heavenwards Thou dost lift Thy holy head
  In praise. But lo! a sword has pierced the breast
  Of Mary. Orient gems no more arrest
Her eyes now fixed upon that Omen dread.
She sees the shadow, but He fronts the sun;
  Sufficient is the evil to the day;
Not yet His silent years of work are done,
  Nor yields the toilsome to the 'dolorous way.'
O sunlit Life, teach me Thy lesson high;
Then, trusting in no shadow, let me die!

MILTON'S PORTRAIT.

<small>ON RECEIVING FROM MY FRIEND, THE REV. A. B. GROSART, LL.D., HIS ENGRAVING OF MILTON IN OLD AGE, BY ALAIS; AFTER FAITHORNE, 1670.*</small>

Grosart, we thank thee, and the cunning hand
  Of the engraver, called by thee to limn
  A face which saw beyond the narrow rim
Of earth's horizon—tranquil, solemn, grand.
What wondrous airs of Paradise have fann'd
  That furrowed brow, what glorious sights made dim
  Those eyes upraised to catch the skirts of Him
Around whose throne the shining seraphs stand.
And as we gaze upon that countenance marr'd,
  E'en as the Master's was, with mortal care,
Affliction, and neglect,—O mighty Bard,
  We learn from thee, if not to sing, to bear—
To work and pray and patiently abide
Till earthly toils and tears are glorified!

<small>* This is a private plate lately engraved by Alais for Dr. Grosart, from which only one hundred impressions have been taken. It forms a companion engraving to Dr. Grosart's Spenser and Marvell and the Chandos Shakespeare, and it follows Faithorne's picture, which is the only authentic one of the poet in old age.</small>

BEECH-LEAVES, SNOW, AND VIOLETS.

To-day I saw fresh violets blow
'Twixt withered leaves and lingering snow,
Autumn above, Winter below,
  With Spring contending:
There lie the beech-leaves brown and sere,
The whiteness of the snow is here,
Between them purple blooms appear,
  Their odours blending.

Thus, yielding not to dead regrets,
Or wintry trouble which besets
The present—like the violets
  Our lives shall borrow

A brightness for the passing hour
From trust in that Almighty Power
Which bids us, like the thriftless flower,
   Fear no to-morrow.

Like Autumn leaves joys pass away,
And storm-clouds vex us day by day,
Present and past have much to say
   Our souls to sadden:
But simple trust will still find grace
To sweeten and adorn its place
And show a calm, contented face
   The world to gladden.

Then let us leave the past behind,
And meet the present with a mind
Which breathes a fragrance on the wind
   Of tribulation:

Care, like unseasonable snow,
Soon melts before the purple glow
Which violets of hope will throw
 Round any station.

SYLVAN AND SACRED.

FLAMBOROUGH LIGHTHOUSE.

As on the beach, moist with an ebbing tide,
Pensive I wandered at the close of day,
I saw a crimson beacon, miles away,
Beam suddenly above the waters wide.
Then chancing to look downwards, I espied
Burning across the sands, a level ray,
Which, moving as I moved, before me lay,
And the low shore with a red glory dyed.
Thus, o'er the rolling ages, lifted high,
The beacon of the Cross afar I see,
And through the misty centuries strain my eye;
But bright reflections from that Crimson Tree
Across the sands of Time stretch sweetly nigh,
Right to my feet, as if for none but me!

AN AUTUMN DAY AT FOUNTAINS' ABBEY.

"A perfect day!" we cried, "A perfect day!"
   As round fair Fountains' winding walks we strayed,
   Where yellowing leaves and mouldering arches made
The valley rich with beautiful decay.
The world-famed jewel of those ruins grey
   Was grandly set in gold and crimson shade;
   The sylvan glories dazzle as they fade;
The crumbling Abbey smiles itself away.
"Alas!" I murmured, "that this earth of ours
   To wasting Time should its perfection owe,
And the brief splendour of autumnal bowers:"
   But down Faith's vista, then I caught the glow
Of fairer landscapes, more enduring towers,
   And deeper, truer joys than mortals know.

ON THE VIEW OF FARINGFORD

(THE POET LAUREATE'S HOME.)

FROM THE DOWN ABOVE FRESHWATER, ISLE OF WIGHT.

From that high down I gained the goodly view
  So long desired—those sheltering groves of pine
  Which round a Poet's home their shades entwine,
Intrusive eyes forbidding to peer through.
Only the curling smoke ascended blue
  Against the dark green umbrage, to define
  The local source of melodies divine,
As ever bard from classic fountains drew.
Much longed I to behold the favoured place,
  O'er which that azure banner beckoning hung;
Those sylvan bowers and garden walks to trace,
  Where many a year our Nightingale had sung;
But then, methought, *that* Songster claims the right
To warble forth his music out of sight!

ON THE NEW CHURCH SPIRE AT GRASBY, IN CONNECTION WITH THE POETRY OF CHARLES TENNYSON TURNER.

Graceful it rises on the green hill-side,
   That fair white spire, and points men to the sky,
   A silent preacher to the casual eye
O'er field and wold and woodland far and wide.
Though but of yesterday, it will abide
   While centuries, like the summer clouds, flit by:
   A landmark, it will lift its head on high,
From age to age the hamlet's crown and pride.
   Meanwhile another structure not of stone,
A life-work built of pure and lofty rhyme,
   Beneath the shadow of that spire has grown
To lend its beauty to the aftertime,
   When Grasby shall assert its kindred claim
   With cherished Grasmere to poetic fame.

TO MRS. CHARLES TENNYSON TURNER.

"Lady," art thou not "elect"—to stand
And daily minister to one so dear,
Who, with his sweet-toned Muse, has won the ear
Of many a loving listener through the land:
Whose Sonnet-lyre, touched with a cunning hand,
Has wakened dulcet echoes, soft and clear,
Destined to wander on from year to year,
Nor ever fail "fit audience" to command.
Well may it all thy pious care engage
Our fragile Songster to defend from harm,
And keep him prisoner in his mortal cage:
That still with measured music he may charm
The cultured sense, till seasonable age
Lays his tired head on an Almighty arm!

TO SOME FRIENDS* ABOUT TO WINTER AT CANEA, IN CRETE.

O happy, flying to the shores of Crete,
  From England to the hundred-citied isle,
  Like the blest birds which follow Summer's smile.
What footprints of Old Time your eyes will meet
Where classic Ida lifts its head to greet
  The clustered Cyclades. What thoughts beguile
  Th' approach to "every city"† mile by mile,
Once tracked by grand Evangelistic feet.
Nor blest alone, but blessing will ye go:
  For on that far-off strand an English home
Shines amid alien flowers, warm with the glow
  Of English hearts, to welcome those who roam:
And oh, what genial hours will o'er ye flow,
  Gazing tow'rds Greece across the Ægean foam.

---

* The Rev. Henry Sandwith, M.A., Vicar of Thorpe Salvin, Notts., and Mrs. Sandwith.   † Titus i. 5.

TO A FRIEND STARTING FOR PALESTINE.

(THE REV. DR. GROSART.)

As birds of passage, in a cage confined,
   When all their mates with one accord agree
   To quit their shattered haunts in bush or tree,
As by a magnet to the South inclined;
Those captives, urged by the same impulse blind,
   Though calm before, now struggle to be free
   And strain tow'rds sunnier lands beyond the sea,
Unvexed by gathering storm and chilling wind.
Such earnest flutterings of desire are mine,
   With thee, dear friend, to wing my southward course,
And range o'er holy fields of Palestine:
   But Duty bars me round with gentle force,
And bids me the instinctive hope resign
   Of tracking Truth's fair stream to its sweet source.

A SYLVAN NOOK,

LONDESBOROUGH PARK.

"Ille terrarum mihi præter omnes
Angulus ridet." HORACE, (Od. ii. 6.)

A grassy hill with beeches crowned
Throws its encircling arms around
My own peculiar nook of ground.

No chilly breath of wandering air
From North or East can touch me there
E'en when the sheltering trees are bare.

There the first violets washed in dew
Come shyly faltering forth to view
And half disclose their glances blue.

And there in turn the spotless May
Puts on her fresh and fair array
And sweetly challenges the day.

Till soon the wild-rose shows his face,
And crown'd with an all-conquering grace
Shines the brief monarch of the place.

And in that sylvan combe are heard
The dulcet notes of many a bird
To vernal mirth and music stirred.

While from deep hidden springs below
Fountains of living water flow
And make soft murmurings as they go;

Then to a peaceful mere expand,
Where patient herons take their stand,
And teal disport, a timid band.

And the swift kingfisher is seen
Flashing its blue and orange sheen
Upon the glassy wave serene.

The silent swan its arch of snow
And mantling pride steers to and fro,
Repeated with a wavering glow;

While coots and moorhens round it play,
And wild ducks light with splash and spray,
And swallows glide and dip all day.

Hither Spring's early birds are blown:
Here through the Summer doves make moan:
And Autumn robin mourns alone.

The fading elms which cluster round
To guard the water's azure bound
Mirror their gold in depths profound.

Each yellow leaf in sunshine sweet
Floats down a phantom-leaf to meet
Through the blue wave upspringing fleet.

And when the beech and elms are bare
The banded spruce stand watching there,
Their changeless verdure imaged fair.

So many charms are here displayed
As if this pleasant place were made
For "a green thought in a green shade."*

The seasons here on circling wing
Reflections bright perforce must bring,
Like flowers that bloom and birds that sing.

On Nature's face who loves to look
In such a calm sequestered nook
Must gather lore from God's fair book.

* Andrew Marvell.

WINTER-BERRIES.

No blossoms now adorn this ruined bower,
    Nor any leaves. The wind relentless blows
    Right through the naked branches, which disclose
The mossy secret plann'd in happier hour
By some fair bird. But Winter has its dower,
    And many a dainty bead and coral shows—
    These clustered berries ruddier than the rose,
And gaily dancing, though the storm-clouds lower.
Thus o'er the leafless boughs bright wings still flutter,
    Nor miss the blossoms mid the fruitage red;
For which sweet voices, silent now, will utter
    Melodious thanks when these dark days are fled:
Oh, may the Winter of my age be found
With timely fruits of ripe experience crowned.

THE ARROW-SEED;

OR, SOWING UNAWARES.

I watched a little bird that unawares
   With all its might was scattering wingèd seed,
   As on a nodding flower it hung to feed.
Loosed by its beak—the breath of Summer airs
Those feathered germs across the meadow bears,
   The while the busy songster takes no heed
   Whither each arrowy wanderer may speed,
Or how in forest or in field it fares.
Ah, we are sowing when we little think
   Wing'd seeds of good or evil all around;
We scatter them e'en when we eat or drink;
   Whene'er we talk they flutter o'er the ground:
Oh, "to the Spirit" let us learn to "sow,"
And from small deeds and words fair flowers will grow!

THE VICTIM AND THE PRIEST.

When as a Lamb, harmless and undefiled,
He faced the High-priest's rage with patience mild,
Though words, like poisoned arrows, did not cease
To fly around Him, "Jesus held His peace."

When to His Judge, who bent a scornful look,
The Jews their bitter accusations took,
And Pilate probed the truth of what he heard
With questions—"He replied to ne'er a word."

When before Herod and his warrior band,
Arrayed in gorgeous robe He takes His stand,
For all the vehement charges that they bring,
"He answered nothing" to the mocking king.

Thus dumb He stood before His shearers all,
And, unresisting, let their fury fall;
No word of self-defence He deigned to wield,
But wore majestic silence as His shield.

As Isaac on the altar speechless lay,
When the knife gleamed to take his life away,
So no excusing voice from Jesus broke
To avert His sorrow or to blunt its stroke.

Long since have vanished priest, and judge, and king,
As troubled dreams at dawn of day take wing;
Their Victim now is on His priestly throne,
And mightiest princes His dominion own.

Silence now seals His gracious lips no more;
He ever lives prevailing words to pour
Into our Father's ear, for each and all
Who at His kingly feet believing fall.

To save Himself no whisper stirred the air,
To save His Church He pours perpetual prayer,
And pleads aloud to yonder listening skies
The virtue of His silent Sacrifice!

THE KINGFISHER;

OR, A HAPPY WEDDING OMEN.

As from God's Book, at matin hour, she sought
  Words strong to soothe a tremulous heart and true,
 A sudden gleam of beauty met her view,
With sweetest promise, like the rainbow, fraught.
A flash of gold, to burnished brightness wrought,
  Shone at her window, and then lightly flew
A living sapphire of resplendent hue,
As if its colour from the sky were caught.
And lo! a voice which whispered in her ear
  Of seas unruffled and of halcyon days,
Serene the future, as the past was dear:
  For "God is Love," and "His are all our ways,"
The golden dawning and the noonday clear,
  And morn to eventide shall utter praise.

THE BIRDS' FIRST HALTING-PLACE.

"Many of the migratory birds make the Devil's Dyke, near Brighton (containing a deep combe, in the Parish of Poynings) their first halt on their arrival from the Continent: but they do not stay long there; they are soon off and away. This locality is warm for them, and probably produces suitable food."—*Brighton Paper*.

Escaped from Ocean's highway rough and loud,
   Our travelled songsters light in this green vale,
   The whitethroat, blackcap, redstart, nightingale—
Like showers of music, cloud succeeding cloud.
In this soft cradle sinks the wearied crowd,
   With panting breasts, and plumes that droop and fail;
   But soon, their ranks reformed, away they sail,
To sweep the land in feathered phalanx proud.
Sweet favoured nook in which to fold your wing,
   Ere, like new Conquerors, ye disperse all round
To seize the groves, and songs triumphant sing:
   Well have ye chosen your first camping ground,
For One* dwells near, a welcome warm to bring
   And with your fame bid hill and dale resound.

* My friend the Rev. T. A. Holland, M.A., Rector of Poynings, Author of "Dryburgh Abbey and Other Poems," and of many beautiful Sonnets on our favourite birds, which have appeared in the 'Animal World,' etc.

BUTTERFLIES.

ON SEEING THE COLLECTION OF BRITISH BUTTERFLIES IN THE CABINETS OF MY FRIEND THE REV. F. O. MORRIS.

In ordered sequence and of rainbow dyes,
  Rank after rank, they passed before my view,
  Our British Butterflies—bright with each hue
Of autumn leaf, fair flower, or sunset skies.
Prismatic tints they flash upon our eyes
  From yonder Light of lights, Divine and true,
  Who lends an insect's wing its gold or blue
Or purple, which all art of man outvies.
Thus yearly have these wingèd blooms unfurled
  Their streaks and stains, each after its own kind,
Since first they fluttered o'er the new-made world—
  Tiny reflections of the Eternal Mind,
Tokens that boundless Beauty reigns above,
Unchanging Order and exhaustless Love.

A TIME OF REFRESHING.
GLEN CRIPESDALE, LOCH SUNART.

I thought to breathe the mountain air,
   But caught a gale from Heaven above,
For lo! the Master met me there
   With gracious waftings of His love.

I thought to hear the ripples lave
   The heathery rocks on Sunart's shore,
But caught the music of a wave
   Which echoes on for evermore.

I thought to hide me in a glen,
   Far from the haunts of busy feet;
But, fairer than the sons of men,
   He showed to me His presence sweet.

I thought with raptured ear to hail
   The thunder of the waterfall,
But heard, behind the silvery veil,
   The still small whisper of His call.

I sought for health and mental power
   To help me in my onward course,
And found an unexpected dower
   Of peace and spiritual force.

I went apart to rest awhile
   From the dull round of daily toil,
And He refreshed me with a smile
   Which turns earth's tasks to golden spoil.

Oh! sweet surprises of His grace—
   To lure us to the eternal hill,
Where He will quite unveil His face,
   And our immortal hopes fulfil!

GLEN CRIPESDALE, LOCH SUNART.

"His voice was as the sound of many waters."

I wander on alone, but not alone,
  'Mid the soft beauties of Glen Cripesdale,
  While murmur'd melodies which never fail
From wooded rock to heathery knoll are thrown:
It is the sound of many waters blown
  Through every nook of this far-reaching vale—
  Rising or falling with the fitful gale,
But always there with its deep monotone.
Oh! that my life, like this fair glen, might be
  Pervaded by the music of Thy voice,
And cheered with gleams of immortality:
  Be this my wisdom, Lord, and happy choice
To listen always only unto Thee,
  And in Thy soothing utterance to rejoice!

ON A HIGHLAND BURYING-PLACE,

IN MORVEN, BY LOCH SUNART.

On Sunart's lonely shore, after long quest
  In vain, embosomed in the hills we found
  An open, undistinguished plot of ground
Where Morven's children take their dreamless rest.
Headstones and cairns are scattered o'er the crest
  Of a green height, with plume-like bracken crowned;
  While pastured sheep repose the dead around,
Who own nor date nor name nor symbol blest.
But kindly Nature watches o'er those graves;
  The mountains fold them in their strong embrace;
Fair Sunart sings to them with soothing waves;
  Soft rains and sunshine bless that burial place:
The shepherd notes it as he wanders by;
And it escapes not the Redeemer's eye.

KINLOCH WATERFALL,

IN MORVEN.

The changeful years have fled and lo! I stand
   Awed by this glorious waterfall once more;
   And Nature's God with heart and lip adore
In this fair shrine bedecked by Nature's hand.
Unaltered are its circling ramparts grand,
   Unchanged the music of its deep-toned roar:
   By the same flowers and ferns 'tis spangled o'er,
By the same roof of azure it is spann'd.
And thus for centuries when I am gone
   This temple will its hallelujahs raise,
These falling waters thunder ceaseless on:
   But what though few and fleeting are my days,
Eternal is the Rock I rest upon,
   And here or yonder I shall sing His praise!

SYLVAN AND SACRED.

LOCH TEACHUS,

BY LOCH SUNART.

A loch, within a loch, girdled all round
  With lofty mountain and with wooded hill,
  Spreads out its silvery waters, lone and still,
Embosomed in tranquillity profound.
Only each day, with a soft lulling sound
  The mighty tides this rocky basin fill,
  And from the grassy uplands many a rill
Brings its fresh tribute with a gladsome bound.
Bright image of a consecrated soul,
  Reposing in the arms of Heavenly Love;
Into its depths what tides of blessing roll,
  What streams of comfort cheer it from above:
While Truth and Faithfulness on either hand,
Like the eternal hills, serenely stand.

THE HIGHLAND SHEPHERD.

Belated on a rough and lonely shore,
    Where trees and heathery crags obscured my way,
    I met a shepherd in the gloaming grey,
And rocks and thickets troubled me no more.
His beckoning form, that moves along before,
    My trusting feet implicitly obey,
    O'er bank and burn; until, through birchen spray,
The friendly lights gleam by the sheltering door.
So, as with faltering steps, through pathways dim,
    This twilight of mortality I trod,
A Shepherd found me, and I clave to Him;
    I wholly trust His love and guiding rod,
And follow, where He leads, with gladsome hymn,
    Until He brings me home to Heaven and God!

THE CROSS AND THE ASPEN TREE,

ASPEN GLEN, LOCH SUNART.

I carved a Cross upon an Aspen tree
   In a lone rocky glen, where nought is heard
   Save tinkling burn or cry of mountain bird,
And where the timorous roe-deer wanders free.
And in the leaves which shivered over me
   The whisper of an ancient legend stirred—
   How on an Aspen hung the dying WORD;
And always since it shudders consciously.
Well might a tremor seize the favoured wood
   Fibre and leaf for ever, which once bore
That sacred Form, thorn-crowned, and red with blood:
   With such sweet sylvan sympathetic lore
My being, heart and action, be imbued,
   And thrill with trembling love for evermore.

THE LIFTING OF THE MIST.

A mist is on the mountain-top, and hides
   The flushing heather with a weeping trail;
   From crag to crag it hangs a cloudy veil,
Which hour by hour immoveable abides.
But lo! the curtain suddenly divides
   To unseen fingers of a gentle gale;
   And purple heather once again we hail,
Decking with beauty the grey mountain-sides.
A mist is on things Heavenly, and the mind
   Labours to see what still eludes its eye,
And fondly feels for what it cannot find:
   Oh, for a gale celestial is our cry
To rend the clouds which baffle us and blind,
   And flash upon us purple Calvary!

MOUNT GLAMAIG, ISLE OF SKYE.

The smoke as of a sacrifice all day
    Crowned green Glamaig, which, like an altar vast,
    Lifts its huge tapering front to meet the blast,
For ever circled with a cloud-wreath grey.
But from the West was flung one parting ray,
    Ere the dim evening into darkness past:
    The altar-smoke burst into flame at last,
And in a blaze of glory died away.
Thus, round Heaven-pointing lives, which altar-wise
    Send up pure incense, gathering mists may rest,
And clouds of various trouble veil their skies:
    But lo! at evening-time they shall be blest;
For them a sunset-glory shall arise,
    And shafts of splendour smite them from the West.

THE GARDEN OF THE SOUL.

Nigh to the place where He was crucified
   A sheltered garden lay,
Where roses hung their heads, with crimson dyed,
   And blushed their lives away,
And lilies of the valley, blanched with fear,
Shook from their silver bells the trembling tear.

And there on terraced rock the vine was seen
   Wandering with quaint festoon,
Or trained with care into an arbour green
   To cool the rays of noon:
Not yet its clusters wooed the ripening sun,
Though the sharp pruning-knife its work had done.

And many a fragrant plant and freckled flower
   Bordered the paths below,
And proffered to the gardener's hand the dower
   Of scent or vernal glow;
While in the shady corners mint and rue
And bitter herbs for humbler uses grew.

Here, where he sat or walked, the rich man made
   A flower-encircled tomb;
And here by loving hands the Lord was laid
   To rest in the green gloom;
And here He woke and threw a charm around
The dewy stillness of that garden-ground.

I have a garden, Lord, to share with Thee—
   Nay, let it all be Thine;
And very near to it is seen the Tree
   Of Sacrifice Divine,
In whose fair shadow Thou canst show Thy face,
And turn to holy ground the lowliest place.

Let my Beloved to His garden come
   And eat His pleasant fruits,
The ripest clusters with the richest bloom
   From off the goodliest shoots;
If any such can grow in this poor soil,
On which my Lord has spent such tears and toil.

But if the fruits of holiness are scant,
   And few its blossoms sweet,
Yet would I find some herb or creeping plant
   To lay at Thy pierced feet—
The hyssop small or penitential rue,
Wet with the tear-drops of the early dew.

Only, O Lord, as in that garden-ground
   Beside the Cross of shame,
May Thy dear presence in my heart be found
   And its glad homage claim;
Nor ever break the seal which Love would place
Upon the secret home of dying Grace!

SONNETS ON THE FATHERS.

IGNATIUS.

From Antioch to Rome with eager feet
   The rugged path of martyrdom he trod:
   Doomed to the lions by an emperor's nod,
The lightning of their eyes he yearned to meet,
And thunder of their throats; for death was sweet
   To one who fain would look upon his God;
   And so with passionate lips he kissed the rod
Lifted at last to make his joy complete.
The tyrant's threatening and the wild beast's roar
   But heralded the music of a Voice,
Waiting to greet him on the peaceful shore:
   His direst anguish was his dearest choice,
Since rending teeth the envious curtain tore,
   And face to face allowed him to rejoice.

POLYCARP.

He looked on those who looked upon the Lord,
   Holding familiar converse with St. John;
   In whom the last soft glow reflected shone
From that sad Face by earth and heaven adored.
In secret cells of memory he stored
   Sweet words and deeds of Christ, and passed them on
   To live in other lips when he was gone,
Sealing the truths our Gospel-books record.
Christ's breath through holy John still breathed on him,
   Fanning his heart's devotion high and higher,
Which not the mists of fivescore years could dim:
   With ardent longings did his soul aspire
Till from a rounded century's utmost rim
   He soared to Heaven on cherub-wings of fire.

JUSTIN MARTYR.

Seeking for goodly pearls from shore to shore,
  A Heavenly Jewel crowned his weary toil,
  And he rejoiced as one who finds great spoil—
Treasure which earth or ocean never bore.
What were the dreams of philosophic lore
  To One sweet human Life without a soil?
  Armed with the simple Cross he now could foil
Singly the dark mythologies of yore.
His wreath of honour nobly did he earn,
  A living "witness" for his dying Lord,
    Wrestling with Jew and Greek in learnèd strife:
Nor shrank he from that last encounter stern,
  The fatal flashing of the Roman sword,
    A dying witness for the Prince of life.

TERTULLIAN.

O fiery Roman spirit—that first bent
   The conqueror's language to the Church's use,
   And where the Eagle ranged the Dove let loose—
How well thy mind befits thy instrument!
In iron warfare was thy lifetime spent
   For facts and doctrines and world-changing views
   Of Truth; the storm, not silence of the dews,
Dear to thy heart and with thy being blent.
And what if, in the fervour of the fight,
   Thy steps might err, through lack of zeal or love
In those who fought beside thee for the Right;
   Still was thine eye fixed on the Lord above,
Still didst thou walk beneath the Father's light,
   And catch the brooding of the mystic Dove.

IRENÆUS.

Three arches of a bridge our faith sustain
O'er two dim centuries to the solid shore,
Where floating myths are possible no more,
And History's clear, unquestioned steps remain.
By three bright links of an unbroken chain—
John, Polycarp, and the industrious lore
Of Irenæus—we are lifted o'er
The chasm, and a steadfast foothold gain.
From his far Western home in Christ-lit Gaul
Our saint could travel back a lifetime's space,
And Orient years in Ephesus recall;
And how his martyred master would retrace
Dear mem'ries which the lips of John let fall,
Sweetly descanting of Incarnate Grace.

ORIGEN.

Close-linked in youth with apostolic men,
    And mighty in the Scriptures, thou didst raise
    A stately fabric of immortal praise,
Based on eternal Truth, wise Origen.
And though we tremble lest thy daring pen
    Venture too near the veil which hides God's ways,
    We crown with evergreen thy restless days,
Thy pious insight and far-reaching ken.
For ivy-like thy busy hand hath wound
    Unfading wreaths about the holy shrine
In which the Oracles of God are found;
    Where Scriptures Old and New their voice combine
Through all the listening ages to resound
    The full-toned thunder of the Word Divine!

EUSEBIUS.

Learnèd, devout, and liberal, he possest
　The heart's love of imperial Constantine;
　Who, dying, whispered of that luminous Sign,
The Cross in heaven with which his eyes were blest;
Of that repeated Vision which addrest
　To his uncertain faith the words divine—
　'With this Cross conquer'—'Let this symbol shine
　glorious standard o'er thy warrior-crest.'
Thus of the Cross above Eusebius told,
　On the blue sky inscribed with golden glow;
But his laborious chronicles unfold
　How that same Cross was writ in blood below,
Until, through pain and prayer and witness bold,
　Earth saw the trampled Church to empire grow.

ATHANASIUS.

When Athanasius faced a frowning world—
   Emperor and priest against the truth arrayed—
   He grasped the precious Pearl, nor felt dismayed,
Though all earth's pride to shake him was unfurled.
What if from his high station he was hurled,
   The jewel of the Faith he ne'er betrayed,
   But kept it, hidden in sepulchral shade,
Or where from hermit's cell the blue smoke curled.
Then, when the storm retired, the triple bow
   Was seen in perfect beauty on the cloud
Each mingling hue defined with clearer glow;
   Thus through dark years of doubt and conflict loud
To one man's strenuous faithfulness we owe
   The Creed to which all after time has bowed.

SNOWDROPS.

White thoughts we bring
Of waking Spring,
And happy bird
To music stirred.

Sweet thoughts we raise
Of those white days,
When Mary mild
Presents her Child.*

High thoughts we tell
With trembling bell—
Earth's Easter day,
Saints' white array.

* Feb. 2nd.

LYRICS:

Glad thoughts are ours
Of angel-bowers,
Where sons of light
Shall walk in white.

THE CROSS AND THE MOSS,

IN THE WEST WINDOW OF MY CHURCH.

I saw red berries and the twinkling gloss
   Of pointed holly leaves, which ordered lay
   On a deep lancet-window's sloping splay;
Where the stern symbol of the ensanguined Cross
Reclined on a green bed of cushioned moss.
   I pondered on the sight. 'Twas Christmas day,
   And the Church smiled in festival array
To welcome Him who counted all things loss
That He might win our souls. Alas! I said—
   'Tis thus we pluck the thorns from the sharp crown
Which pressed upon the Saviour's drooping head:
   We take our cross, and softly lay it down;
We love the Sign and honour it; and there
We leave the burden which we ought to bear.

MY PAINTED WINDOW,

BEING A WEST LANCET-LIGHT IN LONDESBOROUGH CHURCH, OVERSHADOWED BY A BEECH TREE.

No mortal hand, with cunning art, could paint
  My window; for its colour comes and goes
  With the revolving seasons. Now it glows
Bright as the emerald robe of pictured saint:
Now burns like gold: and now, through traceries quaint,
  Sweet sunset-touches of the ruby shows:
  Now the pure whiteness of the Christmas snows,
Or gemmy lustres of the starlight faint.
Like that fair window may my life be seen,
  Rich with successive graces in God's sight;
Now let me serve in manhood's vigour green,
  Now peaceful sink in roseate evening light;
Then upwards soar above yon starry sheen,
  And through the Golden City 'walk in white.'

CHRISTMAS FARE FOR THE BIRDS.

Thanking the God of Harvest we adorn
   The pillars of His House with flowers and leaves,
   And on His Table lay our votive sheaves.
The garlands wither, but we store the corn,
A bounty for the birds on Christmas morn.
   Thus, when the icy hand of Winter weaves
   Its wreaths of snow, and decorates our eaves
With ornaments fantastic and forlorn;
The sheaves we gave to God we give again
   To feed the birds which live beneath His eye,
Raising upon a pole the mystic grain,
   Round which a hundred wings hover and fly;
   While to the God of Grace ascends on high
From men and birds a grateful Christmas strain.

A PRAYER FOR THE NEW YEAR.

Lord, fill my life with service or with song
  To Thee my Master, through the gliding year;
  For daily praises let my voice be clear,
For daily labours let my hands be strong.
Thy sovereign ownership let me not wrong,
  Or that sweet love which cost my Lord so dear;
  Touch Thou my heart and tongue, mine eye and ear,
Let all this breathing frame to Thee belong.
Oh! may the leaves of Life's new volume shine
  With holy thoughts and deeds, like radiant flowers
Meet for the hand and eye of Love Divine:
  So shall they vocal be, like vernal bowers,
With songs of hope, the earnest and the sign
  Of that long Summer* which will soon be ours.

* See Luke xxi. 29—31.

THOUGHTS FOR NEW YEAR'S DAY.

THE CIRCUMCISION OF CHRIST.

On New Year's day the God-sent Name
    Was spoken first o'er the "Young Child,"
His saving errand to proclaim,
    While yet a speechless Babe He smiled;
Jesus—that ear-alluring word,
Jesus—that "joyful sound" was heard.

Thus on the forefront of the year,
    As on the high-priest's brow of yore,
The Name of names is written clear;
    Thus Christ—our Captain—goes before,
And not one day that looks to Him
Can be all desolate or dim.

On New Year's day the "Holy Child"
   Gave the first drops of "precious blood"
From His fair body undefiled;
   Prelude of that atoning flood
Which poured from hands and feet and side,
When as our Paschal Lamb He died.

And thus the sprinkled blood is seen
   Upon the lintel of the year;
Days, weeks, and months flow on serene
   And no destroying angel fear:
For who the humblest soul can harm
That hides behind that crimson charm?

On New Year's day the touch of pain
   Bedewed with tears that Infant's cheek;
He suffered, though He knew no stain—
   Able to weep though not to speak:
Too soon the "Man of sorrows" found
The pangs which crowd this grief-strewn ground.

And thus a glittering crown is worn
   Upon the brow of the New Year,
But it is made of twisted thorn,
   And every point has its own tear:
"Sufficient evil" each day knows,
But "grace sufficient" Christ bestows.

May I each day of this New Year,
   "Look unto Jesus" and be blest;
His Name each day become more dear:
   His Spirit sprinkle on my breast
The blood which quiets every fear,
And brightens every falling tear!

PALM SUNDAY.

"And many spread their garments in the way; and others cut down branches off the trees, and strewed them in the way. And they that went before, and they that followed, cried, saying, Hosanna; Blessed is He that cometh in the Name of the Lord: Hosanna in the highest."—ST. MARK xi. 8—10.

Behold our King in meek array
Comes riding on His prosperous way,
His lips distilling truth and grace,
And pity sitting on His face:
His willing people own the power
That breathes o'er His triumphant hour,
And heavenward drawn by cords of love
In jubilant procession move.

As He rides on His people bring
Their offerings to the Saviour King;
Beneath His feet their garments lay,
And scatter branches in the way:

With praises and hosannas loud
Around Him men and children crowd,
And thus the Lord is borne along
As on a heaving sea of song.

Lord, as Thou passest by this way
My ready tribute I would pay:
The deep-dyed sins which wrap me round
I cast before Thee on the ground,
And like a crimson garment spread,
On which Thy conquering feet may tread;
Knowing for raiment vile of mine
Thou wilt bestow a robe divine.

And Lord, before Thee I would strew
Green branches wet with early dew—
The palm, the olive, and the vine,
A garland sweet for Thee entwine—

All holy aspirations high,
All duties aiming at the sky,
The unction of prevailing prayer,
And praise's cheering clusters rare.

And let me join the marching crowd
That gird Thee with rejoicings loud,
Bringing some loved ones in my train
To wave their boughs and add their strain—
Fair olive-branches clinging near
In dew of youth, an offering dear:
Thus as of old shall children raise
Glad hand and voice to swell Thy praise.

For, Lord, if we should hold our peace,
Earth's adoration would not cease,
The very stones would cry to Thee,
And music flow from every tree.

SYLVAN AND SACRED.

So never shall our lips be dumb
Till to Thy Temple, Lord, we come,
And mingle with the blissful throng
Who raise to Thee the eternal song!

LENT;

OR, THE SHADOW OF THE CROSS.

On a low hill, methought, a Cross I saw
   Lift its dark form athwart the orient sky,
   Where day was breaking in calm majesty—
Azure and gold without one stain or flaw.
From that stern Sign of vindicated Law,
   Which in the sunrise loomed upon mine eye,
   Right o'er the land a shadow seemed to lie,
On which I moved along in silent awe.
Ah, would we bask in Easter's glorious ray,
   Our feet must track the shadow of the Cross,
   Our hearts must count all earthly treasure loss
   And earthly pleasure reckon but as dross;
So shall our Lenten dimness melt away
In the clear light of Resurrection-day!

GOOD FRIDAY.

A COINCIDENCE.

When the Church-tower, at the "third watch" forlorn
   With triple stroke had ushered in the day
   On which the Saviour trod the Dolorous Way,
And meekly climbed for us the hill of scorn;
Lo! the shrill warning of the bird of morn
   Startled the silence, as awake I lay,
   And bade me think how in the twilight grey
Friends joined with foes to wreathe the crown of thorn.
And bird and belfry seemed to me to say,
   'Would'st thou in word or action never grieve
The Lord who died for thee, oh, "watch and pray;"
   That if at midnight, cockcrow, morn, or eve,
The Master comes, robed in divine array,
   His hand for thee a crown of joy may weave.'

EASTER DAY.

"THE LORD IS RISEN INDEED."
"THAT I MAY KNOW HIM, AND THE POWER OF HIS RESURRECTION."

    The Lord is risen indeed!
The chains and bars of Death are swept aside:
Our debt is fully paid, our Surety freed,
    And we are justified.

    The stone is rolled away:
Sin's huge obstruction is no longer seen;
Our manifold transgressions are to-day
    As though they had not been.

    Wide open stands the door:
Eternal Justice smiled, and it was done;
The powers of darkness could prevent no more
    The rising of our Sun.

He shows His glorious face
And scatters mortal shadows with His eye:
Earth is all radiant with the light of grace
    Beneath a cloudless sky.

And still, as years roll round,
Nature prepares to welcome this glad day,
With early blossoms strewn along the ground
    And birds on every spray.

His resurrection power
Oh, may I feel stirring within my soul;
As rising sap through all the vernal bower
    Quickens the sleeping bole.

And oh, may I be seen
Clothed in the glorious robe which justifies,
As now the trees array themselves in green
    To greet the vernal skies.

And let me hear the voice
Of Peace, as of a bird, within my breast,
Which sweetly sings, O weary one, rejoice—
　　His righteousness thy rest.

Be mine the inward seal
To certify my Saviour's crowning Sign,
And make me, not believe alone, but feel
　　That Jesus is Divine.

That He is risen indeed,
The outward proofs are neither few nor dim:
Such witness I accept, but do not need—
　　My heart is risen with Him!

Then let my life display
The Spirit's fruit of self-forgetting love,
That all the world may know from day to day
　　My Treasure is above.

> So, at the Trumpet's sound,
> My slumbering dust Christ's quickening power shall share,
> And rise again immortal from the ground
> To meet Him in the air.

A PRAYER FOR WHITSUNTIDE.

"And Jesus breathed on them, and saith unto them, Receive ye the Holy Ghost."—JOHN xx. 19-22.

The breath from Thy dear mouth,
   Thy Spirit sweet and free,
Is fragrant as the genial South—
   Lord Jesus, breathe on me!

Breathe, Lord, and I shall feel
   Thy peace within my breast;
A balmy gale will o'er me steal
   From Paradise the blest.

Breathe, Lord, and I shall see
   Thy wounded hands and side;
The veil which hid Thy face from me
   Will suddenly divide.

Breathe, Lord, and I shall hear
    The whisper of Thy voice,
Putting to flight my guilty fear
    And bidding me rejoice.

Breathe, Lord, and power will thrill
    This faltering mortal frame,
And clothe me with the steadfast will
    To magnify Thy name.

Lord, breathe upon me now!
    Thy Spirit comes and goes
Like wind upon the fluttering bough—
    Its method no man knows.

But, whence it comes, I know—
    From that dear mouth of Thine:
Oh, hither, hither may it blow
    On this poor heart of mine!

The gift is promised, Lord;
  'Tis pledged as well as free;
I hang upon Thy gracious Word—
  Lord Jesus, breathe on me!

CHRISTMAS DAY.

"Arise, shine, for thy Light is come."—Isaiah lx. 1.

When the Light of lights appeared,
Sudden joy the Orient cheered;
Midnight melted into day,
Winter smiled with roseate ray;
Angel forms illumed the sky,
Flashing on the astonished eye
Of the shepherds watching there
Gleams of glory passing fair.

What, though soon the light which shone—
Crimson mixed with gold—was gone
From the sky and grassy hill;
Yet the brightness lingered still

In that Mother's happy face
Bending o'er the Babe of grace,
Through the windows of whose eyes
Dawned celestial mysteries.

Glory to the Light Divine!
Rise, O weeping earth, and shine.
Bethlehem's Star has put to flight
Shadows of the weary night;
While its golden rays we see
Leading on to Calvary,
Where the colour of the Rose
For a world's salvation glows.

Happy day that saw His birth,
Light and glory of the earth:
Rise, my soul, and shine to Him,
Never let that light grow dim;

Let the world that glory see,
Mirrored evermore in thee;
As the sky retains the glow
When the sun is lost below!

MACHŒRUS.

ENGLISH TRAVELLERS AT THE CASTLE OF MACHŒRUS,
THE SCENE OF JOHN THE BAPTIST'S IMPRISONMENT.

I read* how that dark prison they had found
   Beneath the ruins of Machœrus grey,
   Where John the Baptist languished many a day,
And his bowed head with martyrdom was crowned.
To those thrill'd travellers, methought, all round
   That dungeon dim a glory seemed to play;
   On every stone a tender radiance lay,
In vaulted roof, or walls, or pavèd ground.
For o'er that stonework favoured eyes had pored,
   And honoured feet across that floor had trod;—
Eyes which had gazed with rapture on the Lord,
   Feet which had gone before the Incarnate God;
And Earth's grand Fact more solid seemed and clear,
By means of that stone-vaulted dungeon drear.

      * Canon Tristram's "Land of Moab."

LIVINGSTONE'S LAST PRAYER.

On his bent knees, in attitude of prayer,
   They found him,—those brave Africans; his head
   Bowed low between his hands upon the bed.
They listened, but no voice stirred the night air;
They looked, but saw no motion anywhere;
   Awe struck, they touched him—he was cold and dead;
   His noble spirit up to Heaven had fled,
And left his weary body kneeling there.
And there through all the ages will he kneel,
   As if for his loved Africa to plead;
And with his out-poured hero-life appeal
   To Heaven and earth till God and man give heed;
And that dark continent from East to West,
With rising beams of Gospel light is blest.

ON THE DEATH UPON SNOWDON OF FREDERICK R. WILTON, B.A.,

ST. JOHN'S COLLEGE, CAMBRIDGE, ONE OF THE MASTERS OF THE CITY OF LONDON SCHOOL.

With buoyant step he climbed the mountain side,
   Alone, but not alone, for One* was near
Who made that misty morning bright and clear.
What though no glorious prospect was descried
From Snowdon's brow, but veiling clouds denied
   One glimpse of earthly beauty to appear;
   And erring footsteps down that slope of fear
With awful suddenness began to slide:
The Master whom he loved and served was there,
   To bear his spirit up, and gently show
Visions of beauty infinitely fair,
   And glories unimagined here below.
O favoured youth, to whom the bliss was given
To climb a mountain and to find it—Heaven!

* On his way up the mountain he met with a gentleman, to whom among other things he said, 'I never felt so near to Christ as I do on this mountain to-day.'

AT HIS FEET.

Mary "sat at Jesus' feet," *
Rapt in contemplation sweet,
Gazing up into His face,
Drinking in His words of grace,
By no earthly murmur moved
From the posture that she loved:
Lord, be this my daily choice
At Thy feet to hear Thy voice.

Mary "fell at Jesus' feet"†
When her brother, through the street
By the mourners borne away,
Folded in death's darkness lay;

* Luke x. 39.   † John xi. 32.

All her sorrow forth she sighed,
Christ with answering groans replied:
Lord, in trouble let me fall
At Thy feet and tell Thee all.

Mary stood at Jesus' feet,*
Offering as He sat at meat
Costly gift of spikenard rare,
Glistening tears and flowing hair;
Speechless love and thanks she gave
To the Master strong to save:
Lord, when gladness lights my days
At Thy feet I'll give Thee praise.

At Thy feet once pierced for me
Always shall my station be;
By Thy Spirit and Thy Word
To Thy servant speak, O Lord;

* John xii. 3.

In my sorrow succour bring;
Hear me when Thy praise I sing;
Till 'mid Heaven's high joys at last
At Thy feet my crown I cast!*

* Rev. iv. 11.

THE CHRISTIAN LIFE.

A hand to labour and a heart to love—
   That is my mortal destiny and dower;
   To 'serve my generation,' hour by hour,
And emulate the unselfish joys above;—
A hand to minister, a heart to move
   The hearts of others by the gentle power
   Of sympathy, which opens like a flower,
And soothes all discords like a brooding dove.
A Hand to labour, and a Heart to bleed,
   In Nazareth's workshop and on Calvary's Tree:
Ah, that was God-like sympathy indeed!
   There my example and my hope I see;
A mighty Hand for every human need,
   And a large Heart to bless and use even me!

REVOLVING YEARS.

The years rush on with quick-revolving wheel;
  Like planets round their central sun they fly—
  Obedient to the will of God Most High:
Their crescent orbs to light they now reveal,
And now their face in darkness they conceal.
  This new year, dawning fresh upon the eye,
  Already it begins to hasten by,
And out of sunshine into shadow steal;
But though the years depart, they cannot die—
  "Their works do follow them" in gloom or glow:
The planets leave no tracks upon the sky,
  But the swift years will lasting footsteps show;
  And little words let fall for Christ below
Will send their ripples through Eternity!

SEARCHING THE SCRIPTURES.

Wandering together in the fields Divine,
    We glean among the sheaves, and daily beat
    Out from our store the precious "Corn of Wheat,"
Whose grace and truth for patient seekers shine.
Working together in the sacred mine,
    We trace the veins of ore beneath our feet,
    Till riches unimaginable greet
Our searching eyes, concealed in every line.
Sweet is the Word that "if but two agree"
    Touching some pearl of hope they fain would find,
The rich fulfilment they shall surely see;
    Thus then, Thy promise and our prayer combined,
Shall lead us to the vision, Lord, of Thee,
    And more and more inform us with Thy mind.

SYLVAN AND SACRED.

SONNETS ON THE TYPES.

THE BRAZEN ALTAR.

Fashioned of shining brass, God's Altar stood
   Four-square—its pointed corners raised on high,
   Like lifted hands appealing to the sky
In silence, touched with sacrificial blood.
Here, through the ages, on the typic wood
   A myriad shadows of One Victim lie,
   Feeding the fire which nought could satisfy
Till Calvary quenched it with a crimson flood.
"We have an Altar;" unto which we fly
   Guilty for refuge. Glorious, strong to endure,
By faith we grasp it, and can never die;
   For in God's ear it speaketh mightily
Of One whose sinless life and offering pure
Wrought for our souls a hope Divinely sure.

THE LAVER OR MOLTEN SEA.

A molten sea beneath the open sky,
  With fruit and lilies carved around its rim,
  And filled with crystal water to the brim,
On twelve symbolic oxen is raised high—
Which face the four winds with prophetic eye.
  Is it from sunset clouds that o'er it swim
  The water blushes, or prefiguring Him
Who came to shed His precious blood and die.
Lord, I would bathe me in that crimson sea,
  And leave it, like the lilies, white and fair,
To go about and bring forth fruit for Thee,
  While the dear burden of Thy Name I bear;
With patient labour lifting to the light
The Grace which passes thought in breadth, depth,
    height.

THE GOLDEN CANDLESTICK.

From suns that set or moons that change no light
  Entered the Holy Place; but utter gloom
  Pervaded that mysterious ante-room,
Till from the Candlestick there burst a bright
And sevenfold stream of glory, day and night;
  And, like a lamp that burns within a tomb,
  The golden branches, olive-fed, illume
The darkness with a flame that soothes the sight.
So not from light of Nature but of Grace
  The lamp of Truth, with branches manifold,
Shines brightly in the Church—earth's holy place:
  Oh, may it shed a lustre clear and bold,
The world to illumine and the Lord to greet,
Whene'er we hear approach His priestly feet!

THE TABLE OF SHEWBREAD,

(OR, HEBREW, BREAD OF FACES.)

May gifts of mine encounter that dread Face?
  And will the holy eye of God endure
  My faulty service and account it pure?
Yes, if my life and ordered works I place
Upon the golden Table of His grace:
  Once laid in faith on that foundation sure,
  Of God's approving smile they are secure—
The building precious for its glorious base.
Lord, I would bring Thee not the casual ears
  Of faint desires, but the compacted bread
Of loving labour, godly toils and tears,
  Of consecrated heart and hand and head:
Thus would I live as in Thy presence, Lord,
Thy presence my "exceeding great reward."

THE VEIL OF THE TEMPLE.

The royal purple and the heavenly blue
   With mystic crimson richly intertwine,
   To weave a cunning veil before the shrine
Of glory, all too bright for mortal view.
One only—once a year—may venture through
   That curtain, to behold the Light Divine.
   Not without blood and incense—twofold sign—
In fear he entered and in fear withdrew.
Not yet the way to the Holiest was made plain;
   Not yet on men might Heaven's full glory shine,
Till Christ's last sigh sundered the Veil in twain;
   And now through His rent "flesh" the right is mine
Fearless to pass yon veil of azure hue,
And bask in bliss supreme, eternal, true.

MANNA.

Morn after morn on Paran's grassy floor
   Lay Israel's pearl-like food, celestial, sweet;
   The dew, exhaling, left it at their feet,
Circling their tents up to the very door;
They only stooped to gather it—no more;
   No sowing, reaping, threshing of the wheat—
   The corn of Heaven came down to them complete,
Without their toil or cost, a bounteous store.
Thus spiritual Manna now is shed
   Around our homes, enough for all and each,
Without our labour, in abundance spread;
   Only let Faith her daily hand out-reach
And gather for herself the Living Bread,
   Sweet and refreshing past the power of speech.

THE BRAZEN SERPENT.

I hear a sharp, "exceeding bitter cry;"
  I see a wild and horror-stricken crowd,
  Strong men and children in fierce anguish bow'd—
The writhing limb, drooped head, and filming eye.
I see a symbol strange uplifted high,
  A coilèd serpent, like a banner proud;
  I hear a burst of gladness rising loud,
Responsive to a look of ecstasy.
I see a sinful, suffering, dying world—
  Like ocean, dark with cloud and toss'd with storm;
But lo! a blood-red banner is unfurled,
  Which floats around a gracious, drooping Form:
And through the dimness falls a mighty voice,
"O earth, earth, earth, behold, believe, rejoice!"

THE HYSSOP.

Not to the cedar on the mountain height,
  But to the hyssop springing from the wall;
  Not to a monarch-tree, broad-branched and tall,
But to a lowly herb, fragile and slight,
Is faith compared. Yet hyssop, on that night
  When Death o'er Egypt settled like a pall,
  Shone as the sceptre of the Lord of all,
Outstretched to guard His own with saving might.
Lord, with that sacred hyssop, which could give
  A moment's solace to Thy mortal woe,
Purge me from all my sin, and bid me live,
  And guard and comfort me where'er I go;
I seek not high things like the cedar tree,
The blood-stained hyssop is enough for me.

THE RED HEIFER.

What means that victim in procession led
  Beyond the precincts of the camp, and slain;
  Unmarked by servile yoke or any stain
Discolouring its coat of mystic red?
Soon on that holocaust the fire has fed;
  But stored with care its ashes still remain,
  And dipt in water once and once again,
Like healing dews on souls defiled are shed.
Lord Jesus, who "without the gate" didst make
  Thyself an Offering, crimson, spotless, free,
Now let the finger of Thy Spirit take
  The "water and the blood" and sprinkle me;
And daily show me, treasured in the skies,
The abiding power of the One Sacrifice!

THE SCAPEGOAT.

With solemn voice the white-robed priest confesses
   O'er the devoted Scapegoat Israel's sin;
   While—token of the burden felt within—
With heavy hands upon its head he presses.
The sin-bearer departing, new hope blesses
   The watching, praying host. Straight they begin
   The peacefulness of pardoned guilt to win;
Comfort Divine their thankful heart possesses.
The goat has passed beyond the horizon's rim;
   The guilt is seen to fade away and vanish;
So when the hand of faith we place on Him,
   Who came our myriad sins to blot and banish,
Laid on our Surety's head they disappear,
And all the horizon of the soul is clear.

THE PASCHAL LAMB.

Since Christ, our Passover, for us was slain,
   'Tis our's to keep perpetual "holy day,"
   And with a life-long gladness praise and pray:
For sin is gone, and peace and joy remain.
On the heart's lintel shines the crimson stain
   Which keeps the fatal terror far away;
   Secure we rest by night and work by day,
While justice sleeps, and love and mercy reign.
Oh, worthy, worthy is the Lamb who stood
   A spotless Victim in the sinner's place,
And bought our safety with His innocent blood!
   And precious, precious is the deathless grace
Which gives His flesh to be our daily food,
   As faith's dim path o'er life's drear sands we trace.

"LET US PASS OVER TO THE OTHER SIDE."

"The same day, when the even was come, He saith unto them, 'Let us pass over unto the other side.'"—Mark iv. 35, and Luke viii. 1-22.

The Master, with the Twelve, through Galilee
   The sower's patient toil had duly plied;
Gently He spake, and pointed o'er the sea,
   "Let us pass over to the other side."

A chain of towns girdled the western shore,
   Where Commerce poured her wealth with ceaseless tide,
And footsteps came and went for evermore,
   But lonely stillness crowned "the other side."

Thus oft with wind or oar the Lord withdrew
   From the loud haunts of Labour, Gain, and Pride,
And on those distant mountains, out of view,
   Communed with God upon "the other side."

So, mid the busy scenes of daily life,
   Not always on Care's shore must we abide:
From toil and tumult, weariness and strife,
   "Let us pass over to the other side."

Our home, like Christ's, may be the noisy street,
   But we, like Him, will cross the waters wide,
And climb the heights of meditation sweet,
   Where we shall meet Him on "the other side."

Not to forsake our proper work and place,
   Nor in a selfish solitude to hide,
But to secure fresh freights of heavenly grace,
   "Let us pass over to the other side."

MANSIONS OF HEAVEN AND EARTH.

What pen can paint those "mansions"* brave and
    fine,
  Which sparkle in our Father's House above,
  Where for His saints the hand of sovereign Love
Prepares a place that they may sing and shine.
What pearls and gold and garniture Divine
  Shall meet our wondering gaze where'er we rove;
  What strains more sweet than of earth's happiest
    grove
For our eternal joyance shall combine.
But when the Lord of glory seeks a place
  Below the sky, what temple rich and rare
  For His august abode shall man prepare?
"Give me a heart," He says, "subdued by grace,
  With faith for gold, and tears for jewels fair,
  'And we will come and make our mansion* there.'"

    * The same word in the original—John xiv. 2 & 23.

ON THE MORNING STAR.

In the dim twilight of a Winter morn,
    When the dark earth looks up to the grey sky,
    One radiant Star attracts the wakeful eye,
And sheds a lustre o'er the scene forlorn.
And chiefly as the time when Christ was born
    The Light of a dark world, is drawing nigh,
    You see it hang its sparkling lamp on high,
And with its fairest rays the sky adorn.
I sit and gaze upon its light so cheering,
    Till in the glowing dawn it hides its head,
And the thought rises that sweet sight endearing;
Whatever mortal mists my soul may sadden,
    "I am the Morning Star," my Saviour said,
Earth's dimness with Heaven's dayspring sent to gladden.

HEAVENLY SILENCE.

Above this air we breathe, a mantling bound,
   No hint ascends of thunder's awful roar,
   Shrill wind, or ocean breaking on the shore,
Or the loud battle; but, without a sound,
The balanced orbs fulfil their glorious round
   Through silent depths of space for evermore;
   Like angels prostrate on Heaven's shining floor,
Where, for our discords harsh, no place is found.
Lord, even here such stillness let me gain,
   And o'er the world's disturbing voices rise;
Now let the peace of God within me reign,
   Reflecting the calm order of the skies:
And while beneath my feet earth's noises roll,
Mine be the heavenly silence of the soul.

THE FIRST VIOLET.

Sweet violet, that out of view,
   Through snow and sleet and shower,
Hast kept a speck of heavenly blue
   To bless this vernal hour.

Oh, could we learn thy gentle art
   When trouble clouds our skies,
To cherish in our secret heart
   A hope that never dies!

Sweet violet, that dost enfold
   In buds thy fragrance rare,
Through weary months of rain and cold,
   To sweeten now the air.

Oh, could we emulate thy skill,
    To nurse, through days of gloom,
A patient faith that watches still
    To burst in odorous bloom!

Not always in this wintry world
    Shall Hope neglected lie,
But soon its grace shall be unfurled
    Beneath a fairer sky.

Not always will the breath divine
    Of Faith forgotten be,
But soon a genial day will shine,
    To set its sweetness free.

Then, in serener climes above,
    Shall Faith and Hope appear,
Decking the brow of sovereign Love
    Through the eternal year.

ON THE BAPTISM OF OUR INFANT.

Arrayed in white, we give to God our child,
   While a fair wreath of snowdrops set in moss
   (As lilies might the Laver's rim emboss)
Circles the Font with blossoms undefiled.
From Heaven a white-winged angel is beguiled
   To see his charge signed with the Saviour's Cross,
   Token that he shall count the world but loss
In soldier-service for the Master mild.
Oh, may the "water and the blood" this day,
   Made efficacious by the Spirit's might,
Bedeck our darling's soul in fair array;
   That here a pilgrim he may "walk in white,"
Till, "Well done, faithful one," the Master say,
   "Wear the bright garland of the finished fight!"

MABEL'S HAT.

A little maiden's rustic hat I found
  With hawthorn flowers and oak leaves twined all
    over,
  Golden laburnum, bugle, and red clover.
What though her temples now with sleep were crowned,
As if the slumbrous poppy wreathed them round;
  In dreams she still appears a woodland rover,
  And trips along as happy as a lover,
Through leafy shade and field and pleasure ground.
Thus daily on thy simple life, dear child,
  May Nature leave her fair and fragrant traces;
And daily round thy soul Religion mild
  Entwine the blossoms of celestial graces;
Making thee "holy, harmless, undefiled,"
  And meet to range in bliss through starry spaces.

CRAB-APPLE GATHERERS.

When happy rooks were wheeling overhead,
   A noisy clan—we spent a bright half-hour,
   Children and elders, where, in woodland bower,
The clustered crabs were gleaming rosy red.
'Mid shouts and laughter, soon the fruit lay spread
   Upon the dewy grass, smiling but sour;
   And soon we filled our baskets with the dower
Which Nature from her horn of plenty shed.
Then home we hied, with spoils of Autumn laden,
   And from that fruit a golden syrup drew,
The joy of elders as of boy and maiden,
   At many a merry meal the winter through:
Thrice happy who Life's bitters bravely meet,
And then through grace and patience find them sweet!

HARVEST PRAISE.

Fairer than Summer rose,
A smile of golden glory meets the view;
To right and left, by woodland green it glows,
And by the ocean blue.

Sweeter than Summer bird,
We catch the music of a rippling voice;
With a melodious undertone 'tis heard
To whisper and rejoice.

But soon the standing sheaves
Lift up their hands to heaven and shout aloud:
Like waves at sunset all the landscape heaves
With the exulting crowd.

And at that pleasant sight,
And joyous sound, we smile, and grateful raise
Our song for fields unto the harvest white,
And the Creator praise.

It is the Lord alone
Who calls the tender shoot from the rough clod,
And crowns the springing blade with ear full-grown,
And bids it graceful nod.

'Tis His kind hand that sheds
The rain and sunshine on the yellowing corn,
Until a glittering host of helmèd heads
Each glorious field adorn.

He sends the genial hour
For gathering in the kindly fruits of earth:
He flings abroad the bounteous autumn dower
Of annual harvest mirth.

> Oh, then, let all men lift
> Their heart and voice to God with praises meet;
> But yield their highest thanks for His best gift,
> The dying "Corn of Wheat!"

CHURCH SCULPTURE.

A sculptor I beheld with cunning hand
   From shapeless stone fair leaves and flowers untwine,
   Crowning the columns of a lofty shrine.
Like trees those pillars rise, a noble band,
Their tops of diverse foliage deftly plann'd:
   While oak and maple, sycamore and vine,
   With shamrock, lily, passion-flower combine,
To emulate some sylvan landscape grand.
The God of Nature is the God of Grace:
   Then bring thy leaves, O sculptor, and thy flowers
To shed their woodland beauty o'er this place,
   Fann'd by the breath Divine of holy hours;
Until we almost feel we see His face,
   Whose voice at eve thrilled Eden's leafy bowers!

A CRUCIFORM CHURCH.

(ROTHERHAM.)

Where the far-stretching nave and glorious choir
  With stately transepts, intersecting, blend,
  And form a mighty Cross, I see ascend
As with a leap to Heaven the tapering spire.
It bids me lift my looks and longings higher
  Than this world's smoke and cloud—to let them tend
  To yonder azure Home and gracious Friend,
And set on things above my heart's desire.
Thus, resting on the Cross as on its base,
  See the fair fabric of Religion rise,
Truth her foundation and her topstone Grace:
  Thus ever upwards see her point men's eyes
Which some celestial ladder seem to trace,
  Its foot on earth, its summit in the skies.

WATER TURNED TO WINE.

"'Whate'er He saith to you,'
Whene'er He lifts an eye or waves a hand,
'Servants,' be ready to observe and 'do'
  His first, His least command."

Such was the whispered word
Of Mary, waiting for the Master's "hour,"
Ere yet the Godhead in the manhood stirred,
  To "manifest" its power.

But lo! the failing wine
The rising gladness of the banquet mars;
When, "Fill with water," spake the voice Divine,
  "Yon empty water jars."

It seemed a bootless task;
But clear the order, though the drift was dim;
It was not theirs the meaning strange to ask:
"They filled them to the brim."

Then at His Word they drew
From those full jars, what was not any more
Water, but fragrant scent and purple hue
Of choicest vintage bore.

Oh, fruitful is the toil
Of patient workers for the Lord of grace:
Duty and tears will yield them joyous spoil,
Water to wine give place.

Our daily task may seem
Like pouring water into jars of earth;
But wrought for Him, it wins a roseate gleam
And a celestial worth.

The cup of sorrow pale
Taken from hour to hour by trustful love—
A deepening lustre in it we shall hail,
  Caught from a Face above.

A simple kindness done
To some poor sufferer for the Master's sake,
Like a grey cloud fired by the setting sun,
  Shall into glory break.

Here for a season placed,
As servants we draw water at His will;
There as His guests the new wine we shall taste
  On the Eternal hill!

SOLACE IN SICKNESS.

Clouded with sickness, Lord, languid with pain,
  I cannot work or meditate or pray;
  The night is dreary, and forlorn the day.
From Nature or from Grace I seek in vain
Some gleam of comfort. Shall I not complain
  Of precious golden sands, which slip away
  Out of Time's hour-glass, touched with no sweet ray
Of service, or of spiritual gain?
"Not so!" a Voice replied. "For each dark hour
  Patiently borne, for each sharp pain and ache,
  An added jewel in thy crown shall shake,
And gathered 'weight' accrue to 'Glory's' dower.
  Sufferings are gifts; accept them for My sake,
  And from earth's sighs Heaven's music shall awake."

A SUFFERING CHRISTIAN'S PRAYER.

"My Father, say 'Good night' unto Thy child!"
  And let Thy blessing bring me the repose
  I sorely need, and my tired eyelids close
In balmy slumber and oblivion mild.
Oh, banish evil dreams and fancies wild—
  Sad shadows, it may be, of bygone woes;
  And give me rest—image of peace which flows
Through JESUS from a Father reconciled.
"My Father, say 'Good morning' to Thy child!"
  And let Thy smile bring comfort for the morrow;
Give me a conscience calm and undefiled,
  A courage strong to cope with pain and sorrow;
"The day is Thine," O Lord, "the night is Thine,"
And Thou, through grace and promises, art mine!

THE RAINBOW AT SUNSET.

The Summer-day with cloud and rain was dim,
  And now sinks slowly to its dreary close,
  When, 'neath the leaden canopy, there flows
A stream of splendour from the horizon's rim.
The fields and trees in sudden radiance swim;
  And lo! to southward a fair Rainbow rose,
  Whose braided beauty to the zenith glows,
While birds reviving pour a rapturous hymn.
Long lurked the sun in his pavilion dark,
  To show, at eve, the glory of his face,
And paint a rainbow of the loftiest arc:
  Thus God reserves some kind surprise of grace
Through clouded noons, and to the nearing night,
To lift on high His promised evening light!

HOME AND HEAVEN.

His feet have wandered where loud cataracts foam
   In pine-clad dells; or, through the distance clear,
   White Alps and purple Apennines appear,
Grey classic tower, and air-suspended dome.
O'er earth's famed regions he has loved to roam,
   By palm and pyramid—afar and near;
   But nought now seems to him so fair and dear
As that old Church which marks his Childhood's
   Home.
Thus when our mortal pilgrimage shall cease,
   And eye and ear at length are satisfied
With sights and sounds of earth; oh, what deep peace
   Will rise within us, always to abide,
As that blest "House not made with hands" we see—
Our Home and Temple through eternity!

WINTER LESSONS.

When o'er the naked trees and shuddering air
    Relentless Winter sways his sceptre cold;
Through the rent curtain of the branches bare
    The tapering spire, sky-pointing, we behold.

So, when our drooping lives lose leaf and flower
    Beneath the weight of stern affliction's rod;
That wintry season is the chosen hour
    When praying hearts look up and see their God.

When o'er the withered grass and leaf-strewn ground
    Falls softly the fair mantle of the snow;
Nought but a robe of white is seen around,
    Concealing all the stains of earth below.

So, when our faith, of Heaven-blest sorrow born,
   Takes hold of Christ, His mantle pure and white
Is put upon our souls, and sweetly worn;
   And all our deep-dyed sins are lost to sight.

Summer and Winter, Thou, O Lord, hast made;
   Sunshine and storm combine to work Thy will;
The barren branches and the leafy shade
   Thy purposes of love alike fulfil.

We take our mercies and we give Thee praise
   For all the comfort of the Summer glow:
And through the dimness of our wintry days
   We learn the God-sent lessons of the snow!

A GETHSEMANE MARIGOLD.

A bee crept round my sun-like marigold
  And sucked the nectar from that Eastern bloom,
  Whose shining ancestry did once illume
The sacred olive-garden—where of old
Dark clouds of sorrow o'er the Saviour rolled.
  How strange this honied brightness to that gloom,
  That awful shadow of the Cross and tomb,
That cup of gall and bitterness untold.
O Lord of love, blest Oriental Flower,
  Casting a gleam on this far western isle,
Fain would I seek Thy face from hour to hour,
  To taste Thy sweetness and to feel Thy smile,—
My comfort here, and Plant of rare renown,
My glory yonder, and my golden crown.

ON A CYPRESS FROM MOUNT SINAI,

IN SANDOWN VICARAGE GARDEN, ISLE OF WIGHT.

A seedling from the rugged mountain heights
  Of Sinai, where one lonely Cypress tree
  Sways to the smiting blast, which wanders free
Over those rocky solitudes, and blights
The scanty verdure. Here Love's hand delights
  To tend it amid blossoms, where the bee
  Mingles its music with the whispering sea,
And the Church bell to prayer and praise invites.
O tapering Cypress, my aspiring soul
  In thy symbolic story fain would share;
Not where the stormy blasts of Sinai roll
  May I be found; but in a garden fair,
Where Calvary's Cross and Sharon's rose are seen
Pointing to Paradise and joys serene.

ON A DENARIUS OF TIBERIUS CÆSAR,

THE SILVER 'PENNY' OF THE GOSPELS.

The Roman "penny" in my hand to-day,
   Stamped with the same imperial "image" stern
   And superscription that I here discern,
Once in the open palm of Jesus lay.
I gaze—and centuries, dream-like, fade away;
   The years of that mysterious life return;
   I see the down-turned Face for which saints yearn,
Which dimly floats above them when they pray.
But lo! the silver in that gracious palm,
   Even while I ponder, takes a darker hue;
That Face is marr'd, though still divinely calm,
   That outstretched hand, iron has pierced it through;
Not silver now, or gold, but Gilead's balm
   Of "precious blood" meets my adoring view!

THE TEMPLE WINDOWS.

"CHRIST IN YOU."

"That Christ may dwell in your heart by faith."

Since in the temple of the Christian's heart
   Dwells Jesus, surely through the Christian's eyes
   As through a window, or the thin disguise
Of screen or lattice-work, He will impart
Tokens of His dear presence; and will dart
   Some gentle rays to comfort or make wise
   A weary world that still in darkness lies,
Weighed down by doubts and fears and sorrow's smart.
Is "Christ in us,"—be ours the glorious dower
   To show the Saviour shining in our face,
And through our eyes forth-putting His sweet power
   To help the weak and wayward with His grace;
Oh, let not sin in us those windows dim
Through which the world might catch some glimpse
   of Him.

"MEET FOR THE MASTER'S USE."

"Meet for the Master's use"—
  Be this my guiding star,
Which, to things earthly sitting loose,
  I follow from afar.

I have a Master great,
  His right o'er me supreme,
Who did in love my soul create,
  And with His blood redeem.

He has a use for me—
  A work beneath the sky,
To which, unworthy though I be,
  He calls me from on high.

Lord, at Thy piercèd feet
  In humble prayer I bow;
Oh, make me for Thy service meet,
  And deign to use me now.

Mine eyes are on Thine hands,
  To take each task from Thee,
Till, having lived for Thy commands,
  I die Thy face to see!

THE CURFEW.

'Mid the sweet voices of the vernal year,
   Charming and transient as the flowers of May,
   The solemn Curfew wandered on its way,
And through a thousand song-birds held mine ear.
It seemed to hail me with vibrations clear
   From far off ages, lost in shadows grey,
   When England owned the Norman's iron sway,
Which thrills this bell with a forgotten fear.
So mid the pleasant sounds of earth and time,
   Which sweetly occupy the fleeting hour,
I catch the cadence of a Heavenly chime:
   Full eighteen centuries have felt its power,
As of a bell melodious and sublime,
   Fraught not with fear but Love's eternal dower.

HILDA'S WOOD,*

HACKNESS, NEAR SCARBOROUGH.

In green Hackness, where holy Hilda prayed
  And for her gracious Lord "did what she could,"
  No stone of any building has withstood
The havoc which twelve centuries have made.
Her name has left the valleys where she strayed,
  Low-lying fields, and streamlet's modest flood;
  But, like the setting sun, has caught yon wood,
Which clothes the girdling heights in pleasant shade.
Long as the trees with emerald Spring shall bud,
  Or burn with yellow Autumn, that fair hill
Shall brighten with the memory of the good;
  Her presence vanished, but a glory still
Touches the grove and hallows all the place
Blest by the footsteps of a life of Grace.

* Lady Hilda, the pious and illustrious founder of Whitby Abbey, retired to Hackness in the year 679, and erected a nunnery or cell in that remote valley. The building is quite gone, but its founder's memory lingers in the name given to a wooded hill close by, which is called "Hilda Wood."

ON AN OLD ASH TREE,

NEAR THE SITE OF A FORMER VILLAGE AND DESECRATED CHAPEL IN LONDESBOROUGH PARK.

O ancient ash-tree, shattered, gnarled, contorted,
  But living still, what tales thou hast to tell
  Since in thy shade at call of holy bell,
Hither for prayer the villagers resorted—
Where long the deer have ranged, the lambs disported:
  No cottage smoke now curls from this green dell,
  No chapel lifts its cross; but by the swell
Of falling waters the lone ear is courted.
Man's home and name and memory fade away,
  While still, like hoary Time, this ash survives;
But from the Cross has fallen a cheering ray
  Beyond the limit of these narrow lives;
Not all of man decays before a tree—
We pass—to our immortal destiny!

AUTUMN LEAVES;

OR, "TONGUES IN TREES."

In peaceful solitude they flutter down,
    And strew the sylvan pool and lichened rock;
Deck'd in all shades of orange, red, and brown,
    Which sober green with painted glories mock.

Spring-time can boast its wealth of blossoms fair,
    The Summer umbrage like an emerald glows;
But Autumn's mild decay illumes the air
    With splendours which no other season knows.

Oh, may the hope of my declining hour
    Be seen to brighten with departing breath;
And like the leaves in an autumnal bower
    Take lustre from the gentle touch of Death.

Then, like the leaves, I must my part fulfil
    Through all the passage of Life's fleeting year;
In shine or shade, in stormy days or still,
    At lightsome noontide, or at midnight drear.

Those patient leaves have kept their steadfast place,
    Or only to Æolian music stirred;
Have fanned with cooling shade the traveller's face,
    Or screened the secret of a brooding bird.

And cannot I some helpful influence shed,
    Some shelter offer, or some shadow throw;
Comfort some anxious heart, or aching head,
    While from my grateful lips sweet praises flow?

And as those arching boughs of crimson tint
    Give to the light a beauty not its own;
While through the coloured leaves the sunbeams glint
    On shining water or on mossy stone;

So when my life sinks low on fluttering wing
  May light surround me from the ensanguined Tree,
Through healing leaves a cheering radiance fling
  And bathe my soul in hues of Calvary!

THE BIRD-COMFORTER.

Though from his* sealèd lips, alas, no word,
  On this side Heaven, will ever soothe her ear,
  There lives an echo of his accents dear,
Mixed with the music of a warbling bird;
Which not in vain from day to day had heard,
  In happy vernal hours, his whistle clear,
  But caught the cadence, and repeats it here,
In notes by which a widowed heart is stirred.
Close to the window, in his favourite beech,
  It sits and sings to her, at morn and eve,
And seems, for vanished tones of human speech,
  Some wingèd angel's cheering strains to weave,
Chanting of bowery rest beyond the reach
  Of earth's sharp thorns which mortal bosoms grieve.

* My friend the Rev. G. Braithwaite, of Beechfield, Yealand Conyers, formerly Sub-dean of Chichester, and author of "Sonnets and other Poems." He was a great lover of birds, and could imitate their notes.

HOPE FOR OLD AGE.

SUGGESTED BY THE WORDS OF AN AGED PARISHIONER.

What though the hand of time, with deepening furrow,
   Has graven on my brow full fourscore years,
   And oft my path has led through toils and tears,
Old age is not to me "labour and sorrow."
This tent of mine is shattered, but I borrow
   From failing flesh a brightening hope that cheers;
   And as Life's sinking sun the horizon nears,
I hail the approach of Heaven's eternal morrow.
Not down, but up, the hill with footsteps slow,
   I journey; and behold, a glory rises
In the grey East, which makes my cheek to glow,
   And with strange beauty my dim eye surprises;
Joy dawns; the veil rends; and I see—I see
The Face of Him who opened Heaven for me!

AUBURN.

(BRIDLINGTON BAY.)

A SEASIDE ELEGY.

"Here Auburn stood which was washed away by the Sea."
Map of East Yorkshire.

Here Auburn stood
By pleasant fields surrounded,
Where now for centuries the ocean-flood
With melancholy murmur has resounded.

Here Auburn stood
Where now the sea-bird hovers—
Here stretched the shady lane and sheltering wood,
The twilight haunt of long-forgotten lovers.

The village spire
Here raised its "silent finger,"
Sweet bells were heard and voice of rustic choir,
Where now the pensive chimes of ocean linger.

Dear, white-faced homes
Stood round in happy cluster,
Warm and secure, where the rude breaker foams,
And Winter winds with angry billows bluster.

Here, in still graves,
Reposed the dead of ages:
When lo! with rush of desecrating waves,
Through the green churchyard the loud tempest rages.

Here Auburn stood
Till washed away by ocean,
Whose waters smile to-day in careless mood
O'er its whelmed site, and dance with merry motion.

Here now we stand
'Mid life's dear comforts dwelling:
Soon we shall pass—Oh! for a Saviour's hand
When round our "earthly house" Death's waves are
    swelling.

PARADISE.

Adam all day 'mid odorous garden bowers
  Had lightly toiled—while many a tender word,
  With murmur of the brook and song of bird,
Fell on Eve's ear at work amongst her flowers;
When lo! where grove of pine and cedar towers,
  As with a gentle breeze the leaves are stirred,
  And walking in the garden God is heard,
With voice of love charming those evening hours.
With conscious innocence, and hand in hand
  That goodly pair approach their awful Friend,
Like children with belovèd father stand;
  Then at his feet in adoration bend.—
O golden age! O days of heaven on earth!
When life was piety and labour mirth.

SAMSON'S RIDDLE.

Through Timnath's vineyards as alone he strayed,
    Roused from its secret lair, a lion roared;
    With his bare hands and help from heaven implored,
Lifeless the tawny monster soon he laid.
Passing once more he sought the same green shade,
    When lo! a swarm of bees had strangely stored
    In the bleached skeleton their fragrant hoard,
And there a dainty feast for him had made.
Thus in our path when threatening danger rises,
    Let us trust God and it will disappear;
His Providence assumes alarming guises
    To make us fly to Him, unseen, but near;
While Love prepares a thousand sweet surprises
    God's ways to our weak hearts the more to endear.

ON HEARING THE CHIFF-CHAFF,

THE EARLIEST AND SMALLEST OF OUR MIGRATORY BIRDS.

Where mighty forest trees uprear
   Their leafless boughs on high,
We listen with attentive ear,
   And watch with practised eye;

While music from the loosened throat
   Of many a winter-bird,
In liquid sweetness note on note,
   Through all the wood is heard.

But not the trill of merry thrush,
   Or blackbird's cadence clear,
Or twittering finch, in tree or bush,
   Can satisfy our ear.

Ah, what is that short simple song
    Which trembles through the air?
It is the voice for which we long—
    Our favourite hails us there!

Two syllables are all the store
    Of music in its breast;
But like a fountain running o'er
    Those twin notes never rest.

They tell us that the nightingale
    Will soon be on its way;
And that the swallow without fail
    Will keep its ordered day.

They herald the bright, wingèd crowd
    Which flock from overseas;
They harbinger the concert loud
    Of vernal melodies.

Therefore we love those twin-notes plain
    For more than meets the ear;
As pledges of the glorious strain
    Which crowns the perfect year.

Thus, in our hearts, a still small voice
    Preludes the burst of praise,
Heard where triumphant saints rejoice
    Through Heaven's harmonious days.

ON A THRUSH SINGING AT A FUNERAL IN NOVEMBER.

What means that softly-piped, melodious strain
   While yet long months of chilling frost and snow
   Must intervene before the violets blow,
And April sunshine cheers us after rain?
Of hope it whispers to that mournful train
   Which treads the churchyard path with footsteps slow—
   Of heavenly hope assuring earthly woe
That songs and blooms and rapture yet remain.
Ah, who can tell what bower of Paradise
   May shelter now that dear departed one
Whose praises, like sweet music, softly rise?
   And when the days of waiting all are done
What blissful scenes shall fill our ravished eyes
   While wreathed in flowers the Eternal year shall run!

A THOUGHT IN A MARCH ROOKERY.

With loud content the rook industrious weaves
   The fabric of her nest, while March winds blow,
   And rock the uneasy cradle to and fro,
Curtained by no warm canopy of leaves.
Fostering her callow young ones, she receives
   With patient wing the pelting rain and snow:
   And while her daily food lies spread below,
For future wants and woes she never grieves.
So let us pass through Life's tumultuous hour
   With a light heart and ride upon the breeze,
Trusting our all to that benignant Power,
   Who with a Father's loving eye foresees
Whatever fears may rise or storms may lower,
   Controlling all things with Almighty ease!

PASSING AWAY.

What is the whisper of the dying year?
  "Passing away," it sighs, "Passing away:"
  Nothing below continues in one stay;
All earthly glories fade and disappear.
The haunts to childhood and to memory dear—
  The cherished walls where once we knelt to pray,
  Our very churches crumble and decay:
The touch of Time corrodeth all things here.
But 'mid the general wreck two things endure;
  Nor change shall reach them, nor decay shall wrong;
The steadfast stars may fall; God's Word* stands sure;
  And whoso does God's will,† he shall prolong
His life for ever in those mansions pure,
  Where men shall be as angels bright and strong.

* I. Peter. i. 25.   † I. John, ii. 17.

UNDERSONGS.

Not to the thunder of the mighty sea
  Which on some rocky shore majestic breaks,
  But to the whisper of the stream that takes
Its quiet course along the grassy lea;
Not to the gusty wind which from the tree
  Its wealth of golden tresses rudely shakes,
  But to the gentle-pinioned breeze that wakes
The Summer flowers my harp-strings answer free.
And there are listening ears in these loud days,
  And hearts sequestered from the rushing throng
To catch and welcome Nature's softest lays;
  God made the sweet things as He made the strong:
Not storm and wind alone proclaim His praise,
  But breath of breeze and streamlet's undersong.

THE PILLAR.

"Him that overcometh will I make a pillar in the temple of my God."
Rev. iii. 12.

Shall I a pillar be
   Within Thy Courts above,
Steadfast and beautiful to see,
   And crowned with wreaths of love?

I am a poor weak reed,
   Shaken with every gust;
Thy kind supporting hand I need
   To lift me from the dust.

Yet, Lord, Thou wilt not break
   A reed that bruisèd lies,
But gently raise it up to make
   A pillar in the skies.

Erect it there shall stand,
    Founded upon a Rock;
One column of a beauteous band
    That fear no tempest-shock.

'Tis theirs to rest and shine;
    'Tis theirs to work and bear
The burden of the House divine,
    The Heavenly Temple fair.

Round them what glories blaze,
    What songs harmonious roll,
As myriad tongues uplift the praise
    Which stirs each ransomed soul.

And mid those pillars bright
    The Lord Himself is seen
Walking—the Temple's living Light,
    The Morning Star serene.

O for Almighty Grace,
For overcoming love,
To win for me a pillar's place
In God's great House above!

THE ROMAN CAMP.

AT CAWTHORNE, NEAR PICKERING.

We rested on a green escarpment high,
   Where heather in luxuriant beauty crowned
   A Roman Camp—its deep-trenched foss and mound
Left sixteen centuries since beneath the sky.
From this steep hill the conqueror's eagle eye
   Swept the horizon—hourly glanced around
   The subject dales, the while he paced the ground
With armèd steps where carelessly we lie.
He holds possession in a foreign soil
   And needs—to keep his restless foe at bay—
A vigilant outlook and unceasing toil:
   Thus Grace, in sinful hearts, through life's short day
Must watch and work the native powers to foil,
   And her deep prints no time will wear away.

ON THE SIGHT OF A SEA-BIRD IN APRIL.

Wandering alone in pensive mood, I saw
  A Sea-bird wing its solitary way;
  The sunbeams glistened on its fair array
Of plumage, white as foam, without a flaw.
I felt an admiration mixed with awe,
  Knowing where'er that gentle bird might stray,
  Beneath the shield of England's care it lay,
Protected by the majesty of Law.
And from its wings there glanced a cheering thought,
  For a lone child by a wise God designed:
  'Thou art a creature of a nobler kind,
Thy peace and welfare Heaven itself has sought;
A mightier shield defends thee from above,
Safe by the law of Everlasting love.'

A WHITE CHRISTMAS.

A SONNET FOR CHILDREN.

Dear English children, fresh from happy dreams,
  With Christmas carols blended, what a world
  Of sudden snow before you is unfurled;
How like a dream the altered outlook seems.
Peaceful it shines beneath the morning beams,
  And every spray with beauty is impearled;
  But wildly through the night the storm has whirled,
And sadly on some eyes the cold snow gleams.
While you slept sweetly in the curtained room,
  And blithely woke to welcome Christmas morn;
Children ill-fed, ill-clad, through hours of gloom
  Have sighed, to shudder in the light forlorn.
You darlings—try to soften their sad doom
  For His dear love Who this white day was born!

A LITTLE GIRL AT THE SEASIDE.

Her first evening by the sea,
Oh, how glad she feels and free;
What a freshness in the air—
Joy and beauty everywhere!

How the dancing water glows,
Bridged with gold or streaked with rose;
Golden towards the glorious West,
Roseate where the cloud-tints rest.

Cliffs and crags, how grand and high,
Tower above her to the sky;
And how tempting the bright shore
For young feet to wander o'er.

She could fancy she had wings
As from rock to rock she springs;
She will run and climb all night
In a dreamland of delight.

Ah! dear girl, to such as thee
Life is but a smiling sea,
O'er whose waves Hope gaily throws
Lines of gold or tints of rose.

Life is but a happy strand
Bordered with imaginings grand;
And all eager thou to climb
Up the dangerous rocks of Time.

May the angel-hand of Grace
Help thee o'er each slippery place,
Guide thee on thine upward way,
Year by year and day by day;

And across Life's changeful sea
May it show that Bridge to thee,
Skyward built by One of old
Not with silver or with gold!

THE RAINBOW, A SYMBOL.

When eyes that watched the Flood rise and decline
  First saw the Bow of beauteous colours braided
  Which spann'd a threatening cloud, then slowly faded,
Each heart relied on that assuring Sign.
So when in Christ the dazzling Light Divine
  Spreads out its heavenly splendours, softly-shaded
  In cloud of flesh, our trembling faith is aided
On God's sure truth and mercy to recline.
To see Him once to holy John was given,
  "Clothed in a cloud, a rainbow round His head,"
Earth's fair memorial wearing still in heaven;
And when God looks upon that blessed token
  Encircling "Him who liveth, and was dead,"
He keeps His covenant of peace unbroken.

TAKE UP AND READ.

'Tolle, lege; tolle, lege.'—St. Augustine's *Confess.*, viii. 12.

When light and darkness in his soul contended,
  And sighs and tears forced their impetuous way,
  As prostrate 'neath a fig-tree's shade he lay,
A voice melodious on his ear descended.
It seemed the tongue of men and angels blended;
  Commissioned, with repeated strain, to say,
  'Take up and read,' and soon will shine Truth's day,
'Take up and read,' soon will Sin's night be ended.
Instant he rose, and seized the sacred scroll:
  He reads the words which meet his eager eye,[*]
And God's own finger stamps them on his soul;
  Absolving peace pervades him from on high,
The chains of his besetting sin unroll,
  And leave him clothed with light and liberty.

[*] Rom. xiii. 13, 14.

WINTER WHEAT.

As by some leafless hedge or rustic stile
   Betwixt bare fields I wander, lo, the scene
   Suddenly flushes with an emerald sheen,
Caught from the Winter wheat; a cheery smile
Permitted this dark season to beguile
   With hope of radiant autumn-hours serene:
   As if December wreathed his brow with green,
And whispered through his snows, "A little while."
So in Earth's dreariest Winter-time was seen
   The new-born lustre of our "Corn of wheat;"
   An Infant smile, oh, how divinely sweet;
Blessing the fields those favoured hills between:
And that fair gleam still speaks to Faith's dim eyes
Of Harvest-treasure in the peaceful skies.

WINTER BLOSSOMS.

See how blue violets and the pale primrose
   Round sleeping Winter's brow securely cluster,
   Lending the dreary woods unwonted lustre
Where his recumbent form he idly throws,
While at his feet a shining rivulet flows;
   But soon the Giant will awake and bluster
   Among the creaking trees, and frowning, muster
His icy winds and clouds and muffling snows.
Then with his chilling fingers he will scatter
   The untimely wreath that graced his tangled hair,
Though now the flowers may smile, the sunshine flatter:
Let sanguine Hope give heed to sober Reason—
   Of buds that burst precociously beware—
To everything on earth there is a season.

FROM MY STUDY WINDOW.

(MILFORD HALL, KIRKBY WHARFE, 1863—1866.)

From my Study-window,
   Down a vista green,
In the hazy distance,
   A grey Church-tower is seen;—
Across my quiet garden,
   Between the elm-trees high,
Its dark, shadowy outline
   Stands forth against the sky;—
Across my bowery orchard
   Upon the horizon blue,
O'er field and lane and woodland,
   It terminates the view.

From my Study-window,
  As from Prophet's bower,
Daily I sit gazing
  On that old Church-tower;
While the trains incessant,
  In the distance seen,
Passing and repassing
  Cross that vista green;
And their white smoke curling
  Hides the Church-tower grey
Only for a moment,
  Then vanishes away.

That thin fleeting vapour
  Daily I behold
Blotting out the Church-tower
  Long centuries old:
Like a veil it rises,
  Hanging in the air,

The tower is lost an instant,
   Then again is there:
Thus in that green vista,
   All the livelong day,
Pass the trains incessant,
   Stands the Church-tower grey.

And manifold reflections
   Strike upon my mind:—
In that fleeting vapour
   Man's brief Life I find—
We are here a moment,
   Then no more are seen,
Quickly disappearing
   As if we ne'er had been;
Like that white smoke curling
   In the distance blue,
Floating there an instant,
   Then vanishing from view.

But that Church-tower ancient,
   Standing as of yore,
Steadfast through past ages,
   Strong for ages more,
Seems of Time a symbol
   Gazing on the strife,
The noise and stir unceasing,
   And restlessness of life:
Above the smoke and discord
   Rises that tranquil tower,
As Time looks down serenely
   On Life's brief feverish hour.

Again, as that white vapour
   Conceals the Church-tower grey—
Hangs like a veil before it,
   Then quickly rolls away;
So cloudy mists of Error
   The face of Truth may veil,

And triumph for a moment,
   But Truth can never fail:
The smoke of human systems
   Will vanish into air,
But Truth shall stand for ever,
   Immutable and fair.

At times that distant Church-tower
   Seen clear against the sky
Appears to me to beckon
   My lingering soul on high;
It bids me not to loiter
   In Life's dim avenue,
But seek that far off glory
   Beyond the horizon blue—
Where past Earth's mists and changes
   The Heavenly Temple stands,
Jerusalem the golden,
   The House not made with hands.

Thus from my Study-window
   I gaze with thoughtful eyes,
And gather sacred emblems
   And calmly moralize;
While on the blue horizon,
   Far down the vista green,
That venerable Church-tower
   Against the sky is seen;
And frequent trains resounding
   Across the vista glide,
And with their curling vapour
   The tower a moment hide.

IONA.

I landed on Iona's holy isle,
   And wandered through its ancient ruins bare,
   And felt the great Columba's self was there.
Thirteen long centuries seemed "a little while"
Before the unchanging sea and sky, whose smile
   He knew. He trod these paths; he breathed this air;
   These waves once rolled responsive to his prayer,
Whose murmuring ripples now mine ear beguile.
Nor to the saint alone closer I stand,
   Nearer the Lord I seem, upon this shore;
The solid rock of this historic strand
   Helps me to bridge Time's waste of waters o'er,
And grasp His feet, and feel His loving hand
   In Whom all saints are one for evermore!

OLIVE TREES IN GETHSEMANE.

O ancient Olive trees, into whose shade,
  Chequered with moonlight, the Redeemer stept,
  When, as a lurking lion, the Curse leapt
Upon Him, and our God was prostrate laid;
Here for our sins an Offering He was made,
  And the stern blasts of Justice o'er Him swept;
  Where ofttimes* through the whispering leaves had crept
The breeze of evening while He mused and prayed.
To this still garden-ground the Lord withdrew
  To rest His weary head or bend His knee,
Screened by the hoary boughs from mortal view;
  And here in His mysterious agony,
The grass was wet with an unwonted dew,
  And Peace† sprang up beneath an Olive tree.

* John, xviii. 2; Luke, xxii. 39.   † Col. i. 20.

THE LAST COMMUNION.

A PARISH INCIDENT.

Upon a bed of languishing he lay,
And watched the breaking of the Eternal day:
To cheer his parting soul beside him stood
The Symbols of the Body and the Blood:
With faltering hand he took the sacred Bread,
But from the Wine's rich fruit he shrank with dread;
"Water," he breathed, "let water be the Sign;
The Lord can turn the water into wine!"

WARP AND WOOF.

I mark the insects as in mazy dance
   With twinkling motion up and down they glide;
   While, through the heedless throng, from side to side,
The busy swallows on swift pinions glance.
From right to left the purple foe advance,
   And, true as tilting knights, make havoc wide:
   But still the dancing column is supplied
With eager wings undaunted by mischance.
The air is fragrant with white hawthorn-bloom,
   As here on Nature's warp and woof I gaze
Of mingled life and death, brightness and gloom;
   And when I muse on Earth's perplexing ways,
One thought can sweeten, cheer them, and illume,
   That Love's hand weaves the mystery of our days.

ON A PHOTOGRAPH.

Since through the open window of the eye
   The unconscious secret of the soul we trace,
   And character is written on the face,
In this sun-picture what do we descry?
An artless innocence, and purpose high
   To tread the pleasant paths of truth and grace,
   To tend each flower of Duty in its place,
Smile with the gay and comfort those who sigh.
Dear maiden, let a poet breathe the prayer
   That God may keep thee still, in all thy ways,
Spotless in heart as thou in face art fair;
   And may the gentle current of thy days
Make music even from the stones of care,
   And murmur with an undersong of praise.

SWEET EGLANTINE.*

Sweet Eglantine, whose fragrance rare
Like incense loads the evening air,
  How closely do thy arms entwine
  This forest oak, and like the vine,
Enrich the boughs thy weight that bear.

Such lowly daring I would share,
And hang upon the Strong my care;
  And imitate thy instinct fine,
                Sweet Eglantine.

And there is One who loves to wear
Whatever flowers of praise and prayer
  Crown this dependent life of mine;
  And so I grasp His strength Divine,
Clinging like thee, as on I fare,
                Sweet Eglantine.

* In giving this set of Rondeaux the author thinks it may interest the general reader to know that the Rondeau is an old French form of verse, recently introduced into English literature, and consists of thirteen lines, with only two rhymes, and a refrain composed of the first four words of the poem, which is generally unrhymed.

IN TWILIGHT DIM.

In twilight dim upon a spray
Chanteth a thrush at close of day:
  A chilly mist pervades the air,
  And all things seem of comfort bare,
But Mavis has a secret gay.

What gives such joyance to his lay,
And cheers him with an unseen ray,
  Making the sombre woodland fair,
                  In twilight dim?

Something the opening leaves must say,
Which lends a glow to evening grey:
  Perhaps they whisper, "Have no care,
  Spring's steps are echoing everywhere."
Have *we* no leaves our souls to stay,
                  In twilight dim?

IN SUNSHINE SWEET.

In sunshine sweet the happy bee,
From Winter's weary durance free,
  Hums as it sips the nectar fine
  From golden cups of celandine,
And fills the air with vernal glee.

And yet a sadness creeps o'er me,
Born of that slender minstrelsy,
  A shadow of regret is mine
                In sunshine sweet.

The bee may roam o'er wood and lea,
And murmur blithe round flower and tree,
  But with its music I entwine
  Pathetic thoughts of auld lang syne—
Dear faces I no more shall see
                In sunshine sweet.

DOROTHEA.

(Baptized April 15, 1878.)

As birds in Spring by fresh green leaves
Are welcomed, where the woodland weaves
  A bower for sea-tired wings to rest;
  So careful Love with open breast
Thee, birdie sweet, to earth receives.

Nought here our tender nursling grieves;
No tossing wave of trouble heaves,
  Where thou hast found a happy nest,
          As birds in Spring.

Dear joy in thee our heart achieves,
Sweet Dorothea, and believes
  And names thee God's gift, latest, best;
  Heaven-sent to bless us, and be blest,
And sing beneath our sheltering eaves,
          As birds in Spring.

THE EAST WINDOW IN YORK MINSTER.

Composed after several hours' examination of it with the Hon. and Rev. Canon Forester.

With wondering eyes we sit and gaze
Upon the many-jewelled blaze,
   Where Art has flung her mingled dyes,
   Outrivalling the Orient skies,
Bird, rainbow, flower, and sunset-rays.

This gorgeous mist, this tangled haze
Clears, and unravels, and God's ways
   We see evolve, and purpose wise,
             With wondering eyes.

Sermons in glass the seer portrays;
Seals, trumpets, vials he displays;
   The scroll of time wide open lies,
   Things present, past, and future rise;
God's Book our guide we thrid the maze,
             With wondering eyes.

THE SANCTUARY.

*"Yet will I be unto them as a little sanctuary."—*EZEK. xi. 16.

He rests at peace as in a shrine,
"A little Sanctuary" divine,
  And cheers with song the fleeting hour,
  Like some sweet bird in happy bower,
Where sheltering branches intertwine.

That he is safe he has a sign;
For he is glad though not with wine;
  Filled with the Spirit's grace and power,
            He rests at peace.

Should winds and waves of grief combine
To sprinkle him with smarting brine,
  He murmurs not. He has a tower
  In which to hide when tempests lower,
And since his Sun must ever shine,
            He rests at peace.

"MY FATHER WORKETH HITHERTO."

"My Father works," when the fair flower
With pure lips woos the morning hour;
  Or when the stately wind-kissed tree
  Shakes out her crispèd tresses free;
And the lark climbs his airy tower.

When Night unveils her jewelled dower,
And dazzles with the sense of power
  That circles through infinity,
        "My Father works."

When, ere the storm has ceased to lower,
The painted bow illumes the shower;
  Or marching armies of the sea
  Halt at the sand by God's decree;
In wave, or sky, or woodland bower,
        "My Father works."

BLUE HYACINTHS.

Blue hyacinths with drooping bell,
What happy secret do ye tell
  To all the listening flowers around,
  Which star-like deck the verdant ground,
In sheltered lane and wooded dell?

What merry notes around you swell,
As if the song-birds loved you well,
  And made the echoing groves resound—
            Blue hyacinths.

Your fragrant beauty can dispel
Heart-sorrow for awhile, and quell
  The thorny griefs which here abound;
  For where your glowing hues are found
On earth there falls a heavenly spell,
            Blue hyacinths.

SWEET, SOFT, AND LOW;

OR, THE WILLOW WARBLER.

Sweet, soft, and low, in wood and lane
The Willow Warbler weaves its chain
   Of melody—a plaintive song
   That seems to breathe of ancient wrong
And dimly-recollected pain.

Its melting cadences retain
Your ear again and yet again,
   Through notes more clear and blithe and strong—
         Sweet, soft, and low.

Thus after Life's most happy strain
A minor music will remain,
   Recurring oft and lingering long,
   And heard the gayest scenes among;
Of lost joys hinting not in vain—
         Sweet, soft, and low.

"TILL MY CHANGE COME."

"If a man die, shall he live again? All the days of my appointed time I will wait, till my change come."—Job xiv. 14.

"Till my change come"—with folded wing
My soul will wait its Lord and King,
  While my dust rests in hope below;
  Nor will it heed the sun or snow,
The falling leaf, or flower of Spring.

Above me holy bells will ring,
And birds their roundelays will sing,
  Through the set days of gloom or glow,
      "Till my change come."

The ivy its festoons will bring,
And waving boughs their shadows fling;
  The rain will beat, the wind will blow,
  But oh, in Whom I trust I know,
And my calm soul to Him will cling,
      "Till my change come."

TRANSLATIONS

FROM THE LATIN SACRED POETRY

OF

GEORGE HERBERT.

GEORGE HERBERT'S DESCRIPTION OF HIS MOTHER;*

TRANSLATED FROM THE LATIN OF THE "PARENTALIA."

Holy Cornelias and Sempronias grave,
And all of serious womanhood, I crave
Your tears; for she, who blended what in you
Shines good and beautiful, claims as her due
Your blended sorrows. For this downfall raise
Loud weepings, Dignity, nor lose thy praise:
Stand, Modesty, with locks loose flowing down;
Sorrow is sometimes Beauty's loftiest crown.

The glory of women has perished: and men dread
Lest of each sex with her the dower has fled.

---

* See the Works of George Herbert (4 vols.) in the "Fuller Worthies' Library," edited by my friend the Rev. Dr. Grosart—in which the Latin and Greek poems have been translated for the first time by the Editor and the present Writer.

The fleeting suns she would not wear away
In vanity of dress and self display,
Piling proud structures in the morning hour
Upon her head, rear'd upwards like a tower;
Then spending the long day in talk and laughter—
For tongues' confusion comes tower'd Babel after!
But after modest braiding of her hair,
Such as becomes a matron, wise and fair,
And a brief bath, her freshened mind she brought
To pious duties and heart-healing thought,
Addressing to the Almighty Father's throne
Such warm and earnest prayers as He will own.

Next she goes round her family, assigning
What each may need for garden, distaff, dining.
To everything its time and place are given;
Then are call'd in the tasks at early even.
By a fix'd plan her life and house go on,
By a wise daily calculation:
Sweetness and grace through all her dwelling shine,
Of both first shining in her mind, the sign.

But if at times a great occasion rise,
With visit of some noble, she likewise
Rises, and raises up herself, and vies
With the occasion, and the victory gains.
O what a shower of courteous speech she rains!
Grave pleasantry, grace mix'd with wit is heard;
Fetters and chains she weaves with every word.
Or if some business for the hour should ask,
She glides through turns and windings of the task,
With her replies a match for wisest men.
Then what a mistress was she of the pen!
What graceful writing hers! Mark the fair shell,
Wherein a kernel fairer still may dwell,
The voice and sentiment agreeing well.
Through all the world her well-known letters flit:
Charming right hand, that dust* is all unfit
Where now thou liest, for thy writings fine;
Pactolus' sand sole fitting tomb of thine.

* Alluding probably to the dust sprinkled from a small castor, which was formerly used in letter-writing to dry the ink.

But thou who think'st these things not fitly done,
A mother's praise forbidding to a son,
Away with thy false foolish modesty!
Heartless and silent then shall only I
Be found, when her fine praise rings to the sky?
My mother's urn, is't closed only to me—
Wither'd the herbs and dry the rosemary?
Owe I to her a tongue only to grieve?
Away thou foolish one and give me leave
Shame to forget while pious praise I weave.
Thou shalt be praised for ever, mother mine,
By me, thy sorrowing son; for surely thine
This learning is, which I deriv'd from thee,
Which o'er the page now flows spontaneously,
Its highest fruit of labour seen to attain
In praising thee, though Folly may arraign.

TRANSLATIONS FROM GEORGE HERBERT'S "PASSIO DISCERPTA."*

ON THE REED, CROWN OF THORNS, BENDING THE KNEE, AND PURPLE ROBE.

Vainly ye mock; your scoffs fly wide, vile race;
A Reed in Shepherd's hand finds fitting place:
Vainly ye mock; your pointed thorns may sting,
'So much the more they prove Me a true King:
Vainly ye mock, bending; for unto ME
All times to come shall bend both heart and knee:
Vainly ye mock; if not with purple vest,
Yet purple blood, I claim My kingdom blest.
But if He lives Whom once in sport ye slew—
His life your death—'twill be no play to you!

* A series of Latin Poems on Our Lord's Passion—first discovered and published (with translations) by the Rev. Dr. Grosart. The Latin may be seen in the Aldine Herbert—as well as in the "Fuller Worthies' Library" edition.

ON THE SCOURGE.

O Christ, sole hope of a world scourg'd with woe,
When swelling crimes invite the imminent blow,
Softly apply the scourge once felt by Thee,
Let Thy rod's shadow oft suffice for me:
Deal gently; tender minds their strokes redouble,
And gracious hearts are their own sharpest trouble.

ON THE PARTED GARMENTS.

If, Lord, while Thou art fastened on the Tree,
Thy garments, the accustomed legacy
Of friends, e'en to Thy foes assigned we see;
What to Thy faithful followers wilt Thou give?
Thyself, Thy dying self, that they may live.

ON THE PENITENT THIEF.

And does he now, this robber overbold,
Who largely on his fellows prey'd of old,
Dare craftily assail the very Christ,
To gain possession of the Pearl unpric'd?

ON CHRIST ABOUT TO ASCEND THE CROSS.

Zacchæus, to behold Thee, climb'd a tree;
Now Thou Thyself dost climb that I may see:
The labour chang'd, the toil and sweat are Thine;
While easiness of vision now is mine.
Thus to Sight's measure Thou art seen by all;
Faith only makes or dwarf or giant tall.

CHRIST ON THE CROSS.

Here where the heal'd World's balm distilleth free,
With yearning joy I cling to the drench'd Tree;
E'en as drops fall, sins vanish; nor are they
Half dead,—by Blood's strong gushing borne away.
O Christ, flow always; lest if cease Thy streams,
Returning Guilt no living God Thee deems.

ON THE NAILS.

Whate'er Thou wert, Who lest Thy higher birth
Should take away Thy lower from the earth,
Wast fastened on the Cross, while men made mirth;

Now Thou art mine; I grasp Thee now,—this wood,
These nails, hold fast the Shepherd for my good,
As by His pruning-hook bedewed with blood.

ON THE BOWED HEAD.

Foxes have holes, each bird of air its nest,
All creatures know where they may roost or rest:
Christ has no host to welcome Him; but now
The Cross permits Him His tired head to bow.

THE OPEN GRAVES.

Thy death, my Life, the buried saints awoke,
And for One bound, a crowd to freedom broke.
Thou diest not, but in these drawest breath;
Thy life is prov'd by animated Death.
Seek Him amid the tombs,—He is not dead;
One Cross by many graves is answerèd:
For it becomes not the Lord's majesty
To waste the life He gave, but multiply.

THE RENT ROCKS.

Man was made sound and pure in heart, life, lip,
But Satan shatter'd God's fair workmanship.
When Moses' Law the fragments would refit,
The new-made calf the unmade tablets split.
So when Christ dies, at such a Tragedy
Rocks inaccessible asunder fly:
All things but hearts are broken by Sin's might;
Yet broken hearts make other losses light.

TRANSLATIONS FROM "LUCUS."*

MAN AN IMAGE.

Doubtless I am God's image, but in stone:
This hardness which I feel from sin has grown.
As corals harden from their own beds torn,
Just so does man of native virtues shorn.
Marbles to weep, Almighty, Thou hast taught:
Let not my heart more hard than stone be thought.

THE FATHERLAND.

As a small flame threatens to pierce heaven's face,
Sending up sparks, though keeping its own place;
E'en thus sighs make my soul sharp-pointed grow;
Prayers, hearty prayers, the sparks with which I glow.
The keen soul plies the flesh with ceaseless fire;
'Twill penetrate it, if it does not tire.

* Also by George Herbert, and first published by Dr. Grosart.

ON STEPHEN STONED.

Who strikes a flint draws fire—wondrous to say;
But out of stones Stephen drew Heaven one day.

ON SIMON MAGUS.

Wilt thou buy Christ? Once for us, we are taught,
The Lamb was sold, yet will he not be bought.
Himself bought us; with blood our debts He paid:
For such a price no money can be weighed.
Wilt Thou buy Heaven? Nay, thou hadst better try
What price one star will fetch in yonder sky.
With its own weight curst money downward tends;
Thrown upwards, on your head itself descends.
One only coin to Heaven and Christ is dear;
'Tis that where Christ's own image shines forth clear.

AFFLICTION.

The waves Thou troddest, Lord, against me beat;
Over my head they leap, which bore Thy feet.
If o'er the waves, O Lord, I may not glide,
Yet through them bid me pass safe to Thy side.

ON THE ANGELS.

The Angels' full-grown keen intelligence
Is unlike ours, which needs must call the sense
To give the forms of things; and oft until
The eyes unlock the door and to our mill
Bring corn for grist, unfruitful is the mind,
Out of itself unable aught to grind.
For parted from us by a distance wide
The rivers of enriching knowledge glide;

Unable but through forms of things are we,
By thinking, to find out what ourselves be.
But no such journey need the Angels take
To reach the waters, no such circuit make
To penetrate into what may be known;
Wide open always are their windows thrown.
Themselves they know by method short and clear,
And to themselves both mill and meal appear.

ON A SUNDIAL.

Marriage of Heaven and Earth this dial shows;
Its light to heaven, its shade to earth it owes.
So soul and body are blended in man's frame,
Whose origin from divers regions came.
Think, wretched one, what fears would o'er thee roll,
If earth lacked light, or human flesh a soul.

TO JOHN ON THE BREAST OF CHRIST.

Ah, let me quaff now, thou who drinkest deep:
Unto thyself wilt His whole bosom keep?
Dost intercept the fount open to all?
Nay for me too the poured-out blood did fall;
And thence I claim rights in that breast divine,
And milk roll'd down with blood demand as mine;
Till I, such grace being linked with sin forgiven,
Stay'd on His arm assay God's throne in heaven.

TO THE LORD.

Christ! glory, sweetness, Hybla of the mind,
Heart's crown, where my soul's strife and peace I find;
Nay, let me, let me see Thee, oft I say,
And on Thine eyes expire, my Life,—I pray—

If I may die; or if life is sight-born,
Why, soon to die with prayers, live I forlorn?
Thou Who didst cure the blind, ah, let me see!
Dost deem it sight, when I behold not Thee?
I swear I see not; if Thou forbidd'st this,
With Thine own Face prevent me—and 'tis bliss!

TRANSLATIONS

FROM THE

"EPIGRAMMATA SACRA"

OF

RICHARD CRASHAW.

TRANSLATION'S FROM RICHARD CRASHAW'S "EPIGRAMMATA SACRA."*

THE INFANT CHRIST IS PRESENTED TO THE FATHER IN THE TEMPLE.

Let the lamb go, by hornèd sire to play;
The turtle, with its mate, flee far away:
No need is here of lamb to mediate,
Or tender bird to bear another's fate.
At those poor offerings once, as 'twere, we played
Received by One who much allowance made.
This is a gift the full-voiced boast to wake,
'Take it, O Father, on its merits take.'
A gift, a gift this is, which need not fear
Being fit for God, since God Himself is here.

* See the Complete Works of Richard Crashaw edited by the Rev. Dr. Grosart in the "Fuller Worthies' Library."

ON THE DAY OF THE LORD'S ASCENSION.

Still do we keep Thee here, O Christ, our Love?
Ah, envy much we gain from Heaven above!
But be it so: Heaven is with stars ablaze,
And countless orbs that trick their tremulous rays:
Moon, sun, and coloured clouds, a fleecy store,
By Evening's rosy touch embroider'd o'er.
'Twere little they should leave one light below;
Let one be here, a thousand there may glow.
'Tis vain: since Thou ascendest not on high,
To Thee, O Christ, descends the very sky.

ON THE CLOUD WHICH RECEIVED THE LORD.

O this black cloud; a white breast does it show—
A breast more white than a swan's neck of snow?
More bright than golden sunshine let it be!
However fair itself, 'tis black to me.

From blacker cloud ne'er issued stormy blast,
Nor thunderbolts of angry heaven were cast.
Black! though no showers or shadows round it play;
If night it bring not, yet it takes our Day.

ON THE DESCENT OF THE HOLY SPIRIT.

What sweetest cloud comes wafting golden shower?
What gentle raindrops bring their shining dower?
The cloud which stole our flame, our heart's desire,
This very cloud returns with equal fire.
O kindly-mindful cloud, which could not brook
That we should mourn thee with so sad a look!
'Tis well; no other dew had countervailed
That which from earth to heaven was late exhaled.

FROM DESCRIPTION OF HUMAN LIFE.

Happy the man who welcoming each day
With smiles that answer to its fleeting ray,
Pursues with steps serene his purposed way.
The alluring snares peculiar to the age
His soul enslave not, nor his mind engage;
His life with peaceful tenor glides along,
By fav'ring breeezes fann'd and soothed with song;
Inspir'd by Heaven with soul-sustaining force,
Seldom he falls or falters in his course;
But ever as the eddying years roll round,
Bursting through all the perils that abound,
A wise asserter of himself is found.

JESUS CHRIST'S EXPOSTULATION WITH AN UNGRATEFUL WORLD.

I am all fair, yet no one loveth Me;
Noble, yet no one would My servant be;
Rich, yet no suppliant at My gate appears;
Almighty, yet before Me no one fears;
Eternal, I by very few am sought;
Wise am I, yet My counsel goes for nought;
I am the Way, yet by Me walks scarce one;
The Truth, why am I not relied upon?
The Life, yet seldom one My help requires;
The True Light, yet to see Me none desires;
And I am merciful, yet none is known
To place his confidence in Me alone.
Man, if thou perish, 'tis that thou dost choose it;
Salvation I have wrought for thee, O use it!

CHRIST ALL, ALONE, IN ALL THINGS.

(From the Latin of the Earl of Westmoreland, 1648.*)

If to thyself thou wouldst not wanting be,
Take care that Christ is All in all to thee;
And never fear in Christ Alone to find
Enough to fill and satisfy thy mind;
He who in all things would rejoice and sing,
His every action to his Lord must bring.

---

* Dr. Grosart has in the press a careful reprint of Mildmay Fane, Earl of Westmoreland's "Otia Sacra," (1648,) in his Occasional Issues of rare books of our elder literature (50 copies only).

To My Book.

Go tell thy tale to any ear
Which loves the notes resounding clear
  Through sylvan aisle or winding dale;
  Where lilies meet the nightingale
To bless with scent and song the year.

To any heart that holds more dear
The sacred thoughts of saint or seer,
  Embalmed in leaves which never fail,
      Go tell thy tale.

Where souls are sad and homes are drear,
Like flowers or singing-birds appear;
  Breathe comfort to the mourner pale;
  Say to the lowly-wise, All hail;
Thy words are heart-deep; do not fear,—
      Go tell thy tale.

www.ingramcontent.com/pod-product-compliance
Lightning Source LLC
Chambersburg PA
CBHW021812230426
43669CB00008B/728